EAVESDROPPING ON MYSELF

NORMAN MACLEAN

NORMAN MACLEAN was born in Glasgow in December 1936 to Hebridean parents: Peigi Bheag, nighean Thormoid Ailein, from Cladach a' Bhaile Shear, North Uist, and Niall Mòr, mac Iain Eoghainn Ruaidh, from 'The Green' on the island of Tiree. Brought up in Glasgow, he was evacuated during the Second World War and spent some of his formative years in both *Strathan* at the head of Loch Arkaig and in *Grìminis*, Benbecula. Maclean who is best known as a stand-up comedian, singer and piper, is also an accomplished writer in both English and Gaelic. In *Eavesdropping on Myself* he chronicles his boyhood in Glasgow and explores the push-pull of two cultures: working-class Glaswegian and first-generation Hebridean.

EAVESDROPPING ON MYSELF

An Outsider's Boyhood in Glasgow

NORMAN MACLEAN

GRACE NOTE PUBLICATIONS
OCHTERTYRE

Eavesdropping on Myself: An Outsider's Boyhood in Glasgow
first published by Grace Note Publications, 2015
books@gracenotereading.co.uk
www.gracenotepublications.co.uk

ISBN 978-1-907676-71-0

For all the women called Peigi who have nurtured,
comforted and bullied me throughout my entire life.
The dearest to me is, without doubt, my mother
Peigi Bheag, nighean Thormoid Ailein

Bho d' bhilean thàinig beatha agus lugh,
Bho d' shùilean fhuair mi subhachas nach gèill
Gu saoghal nan saoghal. 'N e dòchas falamh faoin
A th'ann gun cluinn mi thu an gaoth nan speur?

'From your lips came life and strength,
From your eyes I gained joy that will not be given up
Until the end of time. Is it an empty, foolish thought
That I shall hear you in heaven's winds?'

Akhenaten's Last Blessing (1350 B.C.) translated into Gaelic from the Ancient Greek by Uisdean Laing (South Uist) and appropriated by the author as a declaration of love for his mother.

CONTENTS

KITCHEN

I am three and a half years old and I'm standing on the scrubbed white wooden worktop situated to the left of a marble sink. Through the sole window in the kitchen of our family 'hoose' – never 'flat' – two-stairs up at 191 Brand Street, Glasgow SW1, I gaze in wonder at the scene down below.

Shìorraidh, tha saoghal eile air leth a-muigh an sin, Gosh, there's a whole other world out there!

My mother has her hands on my waist, occasionally lifting me up five or six inches to allow me to see more clearly activities in the backcourt two floors below. The 'back' is a rectangle of black, hard-packed earth bounded on four sides by blocks of red brick tenements, each three storeys tall and, I establish much later, containing four entrances or 'closes' on the two parallel longer sides and three on the two shorter ones. Our close was the central one in the short northerly leg. From our kitchen window, forty feet above ground level, I view the sturdy little flat-roofed semi-detached buildings, each with their red terra-cotta chimneys, around four of which were dotted throughout the courtyard.

"*Cò tha a' fuireach anns na taighean beaga sin*, Who lives in these wee houses?" I ask my mother.

"*Chan eil duine*, Nobody," she replies.

"*Dè*, What?"

She explains at great length, in Gaelic, that these are not dwelling places for humans, but are 'Wash Houses' used by tenants of the entire fourteen 'closes' according to a strict rota when the womenfolk in a designated household would rise early and stoke fires beneath massive boilers in preparation for the boiling of bed linen and clothing.

Down to our left a woman in brightly coloured overall with white buttons emerges from the back close next to ours. On her head she wears a white muslin length of cloth wrapped tightly two or three times round her head. This strange headgear attracted my attention because it draws the light brown skin around her eyes and cheeks very tight. Her mouth is a scarlet gash. My own mother's lips are pale pink and I know when she takes me out for a walk on the nearby streets she always has a little black hat in the shape of a pillbox perched on her dark curly hair.

"*Cò tha sin*, Who's that?' I ask.

"*Sin Magaidh Ramsay*, That's Maggie Ramsay."

"*Magaidh … Ram … a … say*," I stutter out the unfamiliar surname. I am accustomed to people being identified by their patronymics, like *Anna Cheit Uilleim à Creag Ghoraidh*, Anne daughter of Kate daughter of William from Creagorry or *Maoldomhnaich Iain Bhàin à Port Pheadair*, Ludovic son of Fair John from Peter's Port or *Màiri Fhraochain à Loch a' Chàrnain*, Mary daughter of 'Heather-Top' from Loch Carnan.

"Ramsay," my mother repeats slowly.

"'*N ann à Uibhist tha ise cuideachd*, Is she from Uist too?" I say, turning my head towards her.

"*Chan ann gu dearbh*, No indeed!" my mother barks abruptly, curling her upper lip and showing her teeth. Sensing that her vehement denial has perhaps frightened me, she pulls me from behind and whispers quietly but insistently in my ear. "Maggie

Ramsay is not one of us," she says in Gaelic. "She belongs to the 'stranger people' – *an fheadhainn Ghallda* – and she's come here to Ibrox from Eaglesham Street in the Plantation district of Govan."

I have no idea where Plantation is, but I know that it is a bad place. I am in a good place. Maggie has bettered herself by coming among us. My mother's dismissal has implanted in my young brain the thought that there exists out there another, surely inferior, race known as the 'stranger people'.

"*Tha dithis aig Magaidh*, Maggie has two kids," my mother says. "The wee girl, Mary's her name, she had in Plantation before she got married and she's known as a Ramsay. Her wee boy – he's about your age – is called Jackie Williams. She had him to the guy from Hartlepool in the north of England she's now married to." This detailing of lineage and geography is not exceptional. Visitors to our house, *Bean a' Chaiptein*, Mrs Smith from Bayble, Lewis, *Bean Sheumais an Ilich*, Mrs Jimmy Martin from Port Charlotte, Islay, for example, all arrive with specific genealogical and geographical details. What is cauterised on my own mind is the notion that 'the stranger people' are not like us, *Na Gàidheil*, the Gaelic-speaking tribe to which I, Norman Hector MacKinnon Maclean, indubitably belong. This is the dawning within me of a sense of 'otherness' that has still to be extinguished.

The stimulus for all these jumbled thoughts, the bold Maggie, is now performing strange actions. From a hank of rope wound round her upper left arm she detaches a length of about six feet, loops it around an iron hook embedded in the tenement wall a couple of feet above her head and with a succession of twists and tugs secures one end of the coiled rope to our building. Smoothly she reels out a single line until she reaches the wall of the nearest wash-house. With a shrug of her left shoulder she shucks the remains of the hank into her right hand. She swings the loops of rope backwards and forwards half a dozen times to gain momentum and, suddenly, without warning, she releases the hank, which loops over the flat roof of the wash-house and round its stubby chimney. She tugs the line tight and by executing a series of neat little lobbing motions with the remains of the hank she has now a taught line of rope, fifteen feet long and about six feet above the ground. Turning swiftly on her blanco'd plimsoles she re-enters her close. Before disappearing in the gloom she turns and looks back with what seems to me to be gleeful satisfaction at her work.

Within the minute she's back. She emerges from her back close, strangely encumbered. She has her children with her. They are wrapped in closely woven blankets of a dun colour that are arranged to cover not only their entire bodies but also their heads. One child dangles down her front and the other hangs down her back. How she manages to carry two infants with only her left hand, the raised arm bent at the elbow, placed casually at the conjunction of the two bundles is unclear. I seek clarity from *Peigi Bheag*.

"*Ciamar*, How . . ?"

"*Isd*, Quiet!"

"*Ach-*"

"*Fan gus am faic thu seo*, Wait till you see this," my mother says, smiling.

"*De rud*, What thing?"

"*Chì thu ruidhle bòidheach an ceartuair*, You'll see some bonnie dance steps very soon."

"*An dèan a' chlann dannsa cuideachd*, Will the children dance too?" I eagerly ask.

"*Cò a' chlann*, What children?"

"*An gille 's an nighean a thug i a-mach air a gualainn*, The boy and the girl she carried out on her shoulder."

My mother turns me round and tilts her head. She gives me a look combining incredulity with alarm. This is a look she will continue to give me regularly for the rest of her life. Her eyes widen and she utters each syllable of each word slowly and deliberately.

"*Chan eil clann còmhla rithe ann*, There are no children along with her at all."

"*Tha iad ann*, They are there."

"No."

"Yes."

No children."

"Over her shoulder."

Peigi Bheag inhales quickly.

"*Eist rium-sa, a Thormoid*, Listen to me, Norman," she says. "What Maggie is carrying over her shoulder is ..." She pauses and points downwards with an extended forefinger. "It's a carpet, just like the square I'm standing on just now."

I make no comment on this information – only maybe an insolent roll of the eyes – and turn towards the window to confirm that *Peigi Bheag* is correct.

Maggie Ramsay has draped a predominately orange and brown carpet over the taut washing line in such a way that both halves hang about two feet above the hard packed dirt of the court. Leisurely she strolls towards the back close. In an instant she returns with a thin column of pleated cane around four feet in length crowned with a flat, circular business end. Maintaining a two-handed grip on what is to me a new tool, she brandishes it at waist level parallel to the ground, gently causing it to wiggle slightly.

Showtime. She takes four steps forward at a fairly fast pace, slides on the sole of her right foot, executes a step-over with her left foot and with a little kick backwards with her right foot delivers a mighty forehand smash with the cane implement to the centre of the hanging carpet. Thunk! Clouds of dust rise. Maggie's crimson lips part to reveal a cruel smile so wide that it almost looks as if it hurts. She strides confidently to the other side. I see the same nervous preliminary shuffle, four quick steps forward, slide, left foot over right, little back kick, powerful two-handed forehand smash: dull thunk sound; rising dust. She crosses to the other side and performs the same ritual with the same resultant climax. Thunk! The display lasts for most of the afternoon.

My mother describes this activity as 'beating the carpets' but, young as I am, I sense that something deeper is going on here. The tricky footwork and excellent hand-eye co-ordination is a credential she is presenting to the world, or at least the world of our tenement. She is telling us that not only is she as good a housekeeper as any of the snobby women who look down on her, but that she is also not a person to be messed with. She's from the Plantation and proud of it. I watch her lashing the carpet with her beater; it occurs to me that some members of the 'stranger people', *an fheadhainn Ghallda*, have a propensity for violence. Though I didn't know it at the time, I would spend a long period of my boyhood trying to insinuate myself into their ranks. I was strongly attracted to the values and culture of working-class Glaswegians. Their socialistic political stance, their lack of deference to authority figures and their willingness to settle differences of opinion by resorting to fisticuffs, all these perceived attributes were terrifically attractive to me in my *fichead bliadhna a' fàs*, twenty years a-growing, period of my life.

OTHERNESS

Our backcourt falls into silence. The quality of the silence starts to change. It becomes darker, more ominous, until it becomes clear that what I can hear isn't silence at all but the low drone of an approaching vehicle. It comes from the interior of a close far away to my right. Three boys emerge into the backcourt. The youngest, barely of school age, has a shock of long, unruly blonde hair and is sitting crouched on his knees inside an old pram. His hands are clamped on the sides of the carriage and his mouth, raised heavenwards, is agape in ecstasy or fear. Two older lads have their hands on either side of the horizontal pram handle; they push and pull the pram with its young cargo forwards and backwards, their mouths mimicking the sounds of a revving engine.

An older boy barks out a command and the pram takes off, propelled by two sets of arms. The pram picks up speed along the straight line that forms the far side of our quadrangle. The blonde boy is squealing with joy. The pushers are whooping with delight. They do not slow down as they approach the left turn they must make if they are to continue their triumphal progress along the perimeter of the tenement block. Oh, they are good these young 'stranger people'. They are perfection, harmony, young and lithe, fast, as my mother described them, like *'fèidh a' tearnadh na beinne*, deer fleeing down the mountain.' On no perceptible signal the older boys stop dead in their tracks. The boy nearer to us stretches forward on his toes and pushes the pram handle forcibly. His partner at the other side of the handle rocks back on his heels and pulls mightily. The rear wheels of the pram scratch on the black earth and a fresh course is set. They're off again. The pace picks up as the pram races towards our stretch of the tenement block. Black sandshoes, or 'sannies' as I later learned to call them, are padding and scratching on the dirt. The boys drive so hard, bare legs pumping furiously, with ridiculous beauty. The young blonde passenger reaches into the air with both hands and shouts something unintelligible towards the very window where I am standing with my mother's hands on either side of my waist. The same manoeuvre is performed perfectly: abrupt halt, right-angled slalom, rapid take-off, faster and faster rush to the opposite wall. "*Dallaibh oirbh, illean*! Go, boys!" I commanded under my breath. *Dallaibh oirbh*, Go!

They perform at least four circuits of the backcourt and I am enchanted. I want to be along with these boys. Indeed, I want to be the boy in the speeding pram. I try to express my exhilaration as I half turn towards my mother and point to the source of drama down below. She dismisses my spluttering. "*Sin agad mar a tha an fheadhainn Ghallda*, That's the way the 'foreigner people' are," she says, lifting me down and placing me in a sitting position in the big chair, normally occupied by my father when he came home on leave every six weeks or so. My back is now to the window, the black-leaded oven and fireplace are to my right and before me there stands a wooden cot where I sleep. This bulky piece of apparatus is at a right angle to the recessed bed and to what is known as the 'tallboy', a piece of furniture with a hinged lid on top, a two-door cupboard and a row of drawers down below. This familiar view does not stimulate me.

One minute I'm staring at the hated cot in the kitchen, and the next minute I'm 'ben the room'. Maybe I've scrambled my way out of the big chair and toddled on chubby legs under my own steam out of the kitchen, through the lobby and into the 'room', a living space that replicated the layout of the kitchen exactly, right down to the recessed bed positioned to the right of the entrance and the fireplace in the exact centre of the right hand wall. Furthest away are three windows affording panoramic views of Brand Street and territory to the North. I find myself standing on the lid of a wooden chest looking out the central window.

At the far side of the cobbled street, scattered with horse dung, there is a cluster of peeling wooden shacks with tarred felt roofs. Opposite our bedroom window there is a courtyard with a single dusty rowan tree, protected by a rickety fence. The little shacks housed private cars, though one of them gives shelter to Mr Ottolini's taxi cab. I know this because visitors from Uist, when heading for Queen Street Station to catch the 5.55 train to Mallaig, always availed themselves of his reliable service. One shack with corrugated iron walls painted in bright yellow is the property of Mr McGillivray, a man holding high office in Connell's Freight Yard just to the east of our tenement building. In what my mother contemptuously called *Am Bothan Creamola*, The Creamola Bothy, Mr McGillivray, the only man I have ever seen wearing a suit and tie to go to work, keeps his gleaming Vauxhall saloon, a lustrous black machine with distinctive chrome flutings on either side of the bonnet. Because of my father's acquaintance with this middle-class gentleman – I suspect Big Neil undertook some work which involved splicing wire for this toff, the only private car owner within a radius of a mile from our home – I experience a vicarious thrill whenever I see a labourer from Connell's sponging down the vehicle and then turning the hose on it before wiping it down with a chamois leather cloth.

Behind the ramshackle huts there lies an expanse of sandy soil flanked by thistles, nettles and crabgrass. Six years down the line when my mother and I had finally left Benbecula for good I would learn to call this waste ground 'The Sandy Desert' where epic football games would take place between the Brand Street - Midlock Street gang and a team from the adjacent slum clearance scheme, a group who were seemed impervious to physical pain and who made up for their inferior ball skills and tactical awareness by a willingness to resort to outright fouling. For them, time was an alien concept.

On the cobbled street below me, horse-drawn carts rumble past my vantage point in both directions. The flat beds of these carts either contain many mysterious bulging sacks or are entirely empty. At regular intervals, some heading east towards Lorne School, others making for Whitefield Road in the west, they pass one another. The humans who guided these vehicles, known as 'carters' or 'cairters', all seem to be aged and dressed in layers of dirty clothing topped by bulky raincoats with faded cloth peaked bonnets, known as 'hooker doons'. From a scrunched up position on the left hand side of the cart they casually flick the horse's reins against the beast's hindquarters, with no appreciable increase in pace. Occasionally, however, they lightly whip their charges' backsides with extremely slim switches that they hold upright in clenched right fists. This encourages the horses to break into a trot, which causes the volume of noise from hooves and wheels to increase slightly. In matters of speed and sound the horse-drawn carts, exposed to the elements, are eclipsed by huge motor lorries whose engines roar in protest as their drivers overtake the slower carts by executing wide, extravagant sweeping curves from within their snug cabins.

As I turn my head from side to side, my eye is caught by human movement on the dirt pavement on the opposite side of the street about forty yards to my right. Outside the iron spiked gates of Warren's Garage – a pukka motor repair centre with three hand operated fuel pumps positioned in a concreted forecourt – two very young boys, around five or six, assume the preliminary crouch of sprinters, one leg cocked and the other knee resting on the ground. What can they be waiting for? Very, very slowly the reclining knees rise from the ground. They are looking over their shoulders at something approaching from the east. A horse and cart, the bed of which is so full of hessian sacks that there is barely enough space for the scruffy, decrepit 'cairter' to squeeze into the front left-hand corner, are clopping and churning their way towards Govan in the west. The boys allow the slow-moving vehicle to pass them before they spring into action. The horse, cart and unsuspecting 'cairter' are directly beneath my viewpoint when the boys quickly dart across the cobbled street and converge on the rear of the cart. With the precision of acrobats they grasp the low metal ridge that runs round the entire bed of the cart and swing their bodies forward and upwards until their feet strike the rear axle. Arms full extended and with their bodies almost parallel with the cobbled street three feet below they glide past 191 Brand Street and I feel my heart tightening. They have travelled about fifty yards in this fashion when something strange happens. The cart comes to an abrupt halt. The scruffy old 'cairter' executes a neat one-handed vault from his perch, lands softly with the precision of an Olympic gymnast on the granite pavement and runs swiftly from front to rear. Without pause he flicks his whip at the boys' hands. They release their grip and fall heavily backwards. Though I'm listening like a bat, I cannot make out what the 'cairter' is shouting. I suspect it's *guidheachdan*, swear words or profanity, employed by the 'stranger people' when they're angry.

11

Chan eil am bodach cho slac, The old boy's no slouch!

It's the boys' reaction I find astonishing. They bounce to their feet, place a thumb on their noses and waggle the remaining fingers on the hand vigorously in the direction of the old man. With feet apart they insolently laugh in the face of the irate 'cairter' who brandishes his whip threateningly before heading off to his driver's perch and setting the cart in motion.

Is ann air an dithis ud a tha an aghaidh, That pair have some cheek!

The boys are in high spirits. Their mouths are open and they swing their arms like windmills. They then perform a peculiar hop-kick figure-of-eight movement across the breadth of the street. The two boys whoop their way across and along a short stretch of the street, one clenched fist raised in triumph the other open palm flapping rhythmically, against their open mouths. Whenever they come across a dried-out mound of horse excrement they boldly kick out at it, sending little gold slivers into the air. Oh, those boys were veritable sorcerers. Reaching a smooth red brick wall, about seven feet high, the boys assumed positions where they stand face to face. The taller boy leans back against the wall and with cupped hands forms a cradle at the level of his knees. The shorter boy places a foot inside the hands of his companion and is hoisted upwards until his upper body is draped over the top of the wall. With his left foot scrabbling for purchase on the top of the wall he wriggles his body into an upright position. He is now sitting astride the wall. He shouts to his pal below. The tall partner lunges upward and grabs shorty's right thigh with both hands. The boy on the wall leans far to his left to resist the pull on his thigh while the taller boy slowly bends his left leg until his foot manages to catch the smooth top. Rapidly the little boy stretches his right arm backwards and grabs his mate's ankle pinning it to the upper edge of the wall. The right foot of the taller boy feverishly scrabbles upwards until he is able to heave himself into a sitting position astride the wall directly behind his pal. Responding to some internal cue both boys simultaneously raise their arms in the universal sign for *I am a winner*. I stare at them as if from a spell and experience what I can only describe as Truth. I watch them in awe as they turn their backs to the street, push off from the wall and disappear from view.

O, mar a tha mi air farmad a ghabhail riutha, Oh, how I have come to envy them!

*****

Everywhere around me is still. Then the slow strains of a Gaelic song, *Nan robh mise 's mo rìbhinn chaoibhneil*, fill the air. Two interior doors are now open and the light tenor voice of renowned Gaelic singer Neil MacLean, is issuing from the gramophone, which is positioned next to the radio on the lid of the tallboy in the kitchen.

I turn my head. I see my mother at my side, her arm round my waist. I want to tell her about the antics of the *gillean beaga*, little boys, but she dismisses me with an imperious wave of her forearm. "*Blaigeardan a mhuinntir Ghlaschu*, Ruffians from Glasgow," she spat out. That was the subject closed.

"*A Thormoid*, Norman," she whispered in my ear. "*Am faic thu an soitheach a tha romhad an-drasta*, Can you see that vessel in front of you just now?"

"*Chi*, Yes."

"*Uill, sin far am bi an Letitia ceangailte am-maireach*, Well, that's where the Letitia will be tied up tomorrow."

"*Gu dè tha sa Letitia*, What's the Letitia?"

"*Sin ainm a' bhàta air a bheil t' athair a' seòladh*, That's the name of the ship your father's sailing on.

"*Cuine thig e dhachaigh*, When will he come home?"

"*An ath-oidhch'*, Tomorrow night."

I am only a little squirt, but I remember that Big Neil is huge and he plays a game with me involving an alarm clock. He adjusts the 'big hand' and the 'wee hand' on the face of this timepiece by squeezing little winged screws at the back between gigantic thumb and forefinger..

"*Am bi an gleoc aige,* Will he have the clock with him?"

"*Bithidh, los gun ionnsaich thu mar a dh'innseas tu an uair,* Yes, so that you'll learn how to tell the time"

"*Am bi stòireannan aige mu Aonghas agus Daidh-Dò,* Will he have stories about Angus and Di-Doh?"

"*O, 's e Aeneas is Dido tha thu a' ciallachadh,* Oh, you mean Aeneas and Dido?"

"*Seadh, am fear as a' Ghrèig aig an robh gaol air a' bhànrigh, Daidh-Dò,* Right, the man from Greece who fell in love with the queen, Dido."

"*Tha mi a' creidsinn gun leugh e dhut smodal de ròlaistean às an leabhar 'Tansy and Bubbles in Fable Island',* I'm sure he'll read for you some smatterings of romance from that book 'Tansy and Bubbles in Fable Island'." The Holy Bible and this lavishly illustrated volume of classical tales, bound in dark blue leather, were the only books in our house. The latter came into our possession as a prize in a marketing ploy by one of the city's evening papers. Clip so many coupons from the newspaper, send a bundle to Albion Street and your gift was Tansy and Bubbles.

The final question I ask my mother concerns something that has been irritating me for some time. "*Dè chanas m' athair cho luath 's a chì e mi,* What will my father say as soon as he sees me?"

"*Canaidh e: 'Ciamar a tha am 'boy',* He'll say: 'How's the boy?'"

"*Carson a chanas e 'boy' riumsa,* Why does he call me 'boy'?"

"*Cha robh e fada gu leòr an Sgoil Loch nam Madadh airson Gàidhlig cheart ionnsachadh,* He wasn't in Lochmaddy School long enough to learn proper Gaelic."

"*An e 'boy' am facal a th' aca ann an Tiriodh airson 'gille',* Is 'boy' the word they use in Tiree for 'gille'?"

'S e sin am facal a th' aig t' athair co-dhiù, That's the word your father uses anyway."

There is a long pause. "*A Thormoid,* Norman," she eventually says,"*tha fhios agad gum feum dà chainnt a bhith aig na daoine againn fhin ann an Glaschu – Gàidhlig agus Beurla,* you know our people need two languages in Glasgow – Gaelic and English."

"*'N fhìrinn,* True?"

"*Leig as t'inntinn e an-dràsta,* Forget about it just now," my mother whispers in my ear. "*Dh'fheumadh tu a bhith nad dhearg amadan mura togadh tu a' Bheurla Shasannach gu math ealamh,* You'd have to be a completely dense person not to pick up the English language pretty quickly. *Na diochuimhnich do Ghàidhlig: cha trom i a giùlan,* Don't forget your Gaelic: she's not a heavy burden to carry."

I am happy. My father will come back into my life after only one sleep. My mother, *Peigi Bheag,* is by my side. She is always with me, feeding and cleaning me, keeping me steady as I stand, and now whispering good things softly in my ear.

VIRGIL PITCHES UP IN GOVAN

It is early evening in midwinter 1941 and along with a leather covered book on the table a candle flickers and an old alarm clock lies on its side. My father is dressed in black wool trousers and a pale blue singlet, which shows off his bronzed shoulders, chest, and muscular arms.

"*Fo bhuaidh Iùno agus Bhèanas, diathan beaga a bhiodh na Ròmanaich a' creidsinn annta, thuit Dido, bànrigh Cartago, ann an trom gaol le Aeneas, prionnsa a Tròidh,* Under the influence of Juno and Venus, minor gods whom the Romans worshipped, Dido the queen of Carthage fell madly in love with Aeneas, the Trojan prince," Big Neil recites from the open book before him on the linoleum-covered kitchen table.

With his left arm curled around my lower chest, he keeps his thumb on a plate photograph on the left hand page. I marvel at the thickness of this digit which approximates the girth of my upper arms. The photograph depicts a kind of monochrome seal or medal with a female wolf suckling two naked infants. There are spiky black marks on a white background beneath the plinth on which the animal and the humans are placed.

Neil's right arm is extended to allow him to follow more strange markings on the right hand page with his forefinger. His massive forearm, the legacy of a working life spent wrestling with steel spikes and thick wire in an arcane practice called 'splicing', holds me firm against his mighty chest. I hear the deep rumble of his voice and I wiggle my tiny legs in pleasure as I sit astride his right thigh. From my angle of perception, as a tiny four year old, every feature my father possesses is gigantic. In truth, at six foot four, by the standard of the average Glaswegian adult male at the time, *Niall Mòr* truly is a giant. In his embrace I feel unassailably safe.

He continues the story of Aeneas and Dido: *"Bha an dia mòr Iùpeatair an dèidh òrdugh a thoirt seachad do dh'Aonghas mar thà.* The great god Jupiter had already given an order to Aeneas. *B' fheudar dha seòladh a Tròidh gu ruige An Eadailt los gun stèidhicheadh e baile anns an dùthaich sin air am biodh An Ròimh mar ainm,* He was charged with sailing to Italy to found a township that would become Rome."

The Capstan-cured voice envelopes my entire being and I squirm in delicious anticipation.

A pledge to a superior power is a very important promise, isn't it?

Big Neil resumes his narrative: *"Ach thug aimsir ghailleanach orra cumail ri port ann an Cartago,* but his ships are blown off course and he lands in Carthage first. *Cuiridh Cupid saighead ann am broilleach Dido agus theid i as a ciall leis a' ghaol,* Cupid fires his arrow into Dido's breast and she is ruined by love."

My father speaks in the measured, almost hypnotic tones of an orator blessed with the gift of enthralling any listener. *"Ged nach eil cabhag air Aoghnas a dhol gu muir a-rithis, tha Iùpeatair air teachdaire a chur thuige, tro mheadhan Mercury, a dh'innse dha gu bheil an t-àm aige falbh 's nach urrainn dha fuireach ann an Cartago nas fhaide,* Although Aeneas is not in all that great a hurry to resume his epic journey, Jupiter sends Mercury to tell him that he must leave his queen and Carthage immediately."

Young as I am, I empathise with Aeneas. The vow made to a superior cannot be broken lightly.

Hanging out with Queen Dido may be pleasant, but having a good time is surely trumped by duty, isn't it?

The hero's dilemma summons up a sliver of memory. Despite my mother's repeated imprecations to avoid the values of the 'stranger people', I am strongly attracted by these very same values. Which path will Aeneas take? *"Chuir Aoghnas roimhe gun seòladh an cabhlach aige a chùrsa dhan Eadailt,* Aeneas decided to have his fleet sail to Italy."

There, my father pauses to let the implications of the hero's decision sink in. *"Tha Dido a' tuigsinn gu bheil am fear a bh' ann a' dol ga fàgail, agus tha i a' breith air,* Dido realises that her lover is about to leave her and she corners him." Neil hoists me up a couple of inches to enable to whisper in my ear.

"An innis mi dhut mar a theann i ri chàineadh, Do you want me to tell you how she insulted him?" my father asks slyly.

"O, tha gu dearbh, Oh, definitely," I gasp.

The deep sounds of his voice resonate in my belly. *"An robh dùil agad gum falmhamhaicheadh tu an cron grànda a rinn thu orm-sa, a thrusdair,* Did you think you would hide the evil deed you did to me, traitor? *An robh thu a' dol a theicheadh orm gun rabhadh a thoirt dhomh,* were you about to flee from me without giving me warning? *Nach robh an gaol a bh' eadarainn làidir gu leòr airson do cheangal an sheo,* Was our love not strong enough to keep you tied to this place? *An do dhiochuimhnich thu an gealladh a thug thu dhomh-sa,* Did you forget the vow you made to me? *An e gu bheil e an dàn do Dhido bàs neo-thruacanta mar seo fhaighinn,* Is it Dido's fate to suffer a cruel death like this? *Carson a tha na bàtaichean agaibh a' dèanamh aodaich ann an dùbhlachd a' gheamhraidh,* Why are your ships setting sail in the middle of winter? Nì stoirmean sgrios air a' chabhlach, The fleet will be wrecked by storms. *Tha mi a' guidhe ort gu dùrachdach: fan còmhla rium fhin,* I beseech you earnestly: stay here along with me."

My father's deep baritone increases in volume as he imitates the wrath of Queen Dido. *"Cha b' e ban-dia a bha nad mhàthair, agus cha bhuineadh Dardanus dha do shìnnsearan, a bhreugadair ghrod tha thu ann,* No godess was your mother, and Dardanus was no ancestor of yours. *B' iad creagan cruaidh nam beanntan Caucusus a thug breith dhut, agus 's e tìgeir às Hyrcana a thug an t-sine-deoghail dhut 's tu nad phaiste,* The hard rocks of the Caucusus gave birth to you, and the Hyrcanan tiger suckled you when you were an infant."

Big Neil is almost snarling as he utters these last words. He pauses, then remarks in normal tones, *"Nach e Aeneas a fhuair a mhi-shealbh,* What a telling-off Aeneas got!" His voice softens in preparation for the denouement. I love the way he varies the volume and cadence of his speech. *"'S e dleasdanas a mhaireas,* The call of duty will out."

He pulls me up until the top of my head rests against his throat, *"Foghainnidh siud an-dràsta,* That'll do for now," he murmurs softly. I like this warm breeze wafting by my ears.

"Ach bidh tuilleadh againn am-màireach, nach bi, But we'll have more tomorrow, won't we?"

"Bithidh, a ghràidhein, agus an earair. Than na ficheadan de stòireannan am broinn an leabhair seo, Yes, pet, and the day after. There are scores of stories inside this book."

"Dè mar a gheibh mi thuca, How do I get to them?"

"Ionnsaichidh mise dhut mar a leughas tu iad, I'll teach you how to read them."

"Cuine thòisicheas sinn, When will we start?"

"Nuair a dh'ionnsaicheas tu a' Bheurla, When you learn English."

"Carson a dh'fheumas mi Beurla ionnsachadh, Why do I have to learn English?"

"Oir, tha na sgeulachdan anns an leabhar seo – agus an iomadh leabhar eile – uile air an sgrìobhadh ann am Beurla, Because, the stories in this book – and in many other books – are all written in English."

I think about this for a good minute or two.

"Ciamar tha mi a' dol a dh'ionnsachadh Beurla, How am I going to learn English?"

"Bioraich do chluasan, Prick up your ears."

Still carrying me close to his chest he walks over to the tallboy where the radio sits. He twiddles a knob and a woman's voice wafts out of the speaker.

"Sin agad a' Bheurla, That's English," my father says as he carries me back to the table where he sits on the chair overlooking the enchanted book of mysteries. *"Nuair a theid agad air bruidhinn sa chainnt seo, seallaidh mi dhut mar a tha na faclan air an sgrìobhadh,* When you're able to speak this language, I'll show you how the words are written."

"Agus bidh comas leughaidh agam an uair sin, And I'll be able to read then?"

"Gu deifinne, Absolutely."

I realise in a kind of epiphanic flush that I have discovered a new way of living – through the magic in the pages of a book.

"Ach cuimhnich, a Thormoid," Big Neil says in cautious tones, *"'s e a' Bheurla a bhios tu a' leughadh,* Remember, Norman, you'll be reading in English."

"Chan e an cànan againn fhìn a bhios mi a' leughadh, It's not our language I'll be reading?"

"Chan e, No."

"Mar sin, bha sibh-se a' leughadh ann am Beurla, nach robh, So, you were reading in English, weren't you?"

"Bha, Yes."

"Ach … cha chuala mise ach Gàidhlig, But …all I heard was Gaelic."

"Tha sin ceart, That's right. *'S ann bha mi a' tionndadh na bha mi a' leughadh gu Gàidhlig mar a bha mi a' dol air adhart,* What I was doing was turning what I read into Gaelic as I went along."

I close my eyes. For now I just want to vanish. I feel weak and disadvantaged. Will I ever be able to accomplish this feat? I open my eyes and look up at my father's chin. *"Athair, am bi mise cho math ruib' fhein nuair a dh'fhàsas mi mòr,* Father, do you think I'll ever be as good as you when I grow up?"

"Leigidh mi leat norrag a ghabhail an toiseach, I'm going to let you have a wee sleep just now.

"Ach …"

"'S ann a bhios tu fada nas fheàrr na mise, You'll be a lot better than I ever was.

"Tapadh leibh, Thank you"

I am staring anxiously up at the face of Big Neil. *"Tha miann bàis agam air ionnsachadh mar a leughas mi ann am Beurla,* athair, I'm desperate to learn how to read in English, father," I say.

"Tha fhios agam, I know," my father says. *"Ionnsaichidh tu sin, a Thormoid,* You will learn, Norman. *Ach dèan cadal an dràsta, agus oibrichidh sinn air a' ghleoc nuair a dhùisgeas tu,* But have a wee sleep just now, and we'll work on the clock when you waken up."

On this promise I lean back against the broad chest of my father. I feel the softness of his chest hair against the back of my head. The candle flickers and wavers. The sound of a man's voice speaking in English comes faintly from the radio. I snuggle into the line of Neil's upper body, smell the sweet odour of tobacco spiced with a spirit of some kind – rum or whisky perhaps – and fall asleep.

TRAINING FOR PERFORMANCE

The most important thing I learned as a child was how to be a singer. My teacher is my paternal grandfather from The Green in Tiree, *Iain Eòghainn Ruaidh*. The old man is living for us for a while in our one-bedroom tenement flat in Govan after burying his wife, Flora, on that island. I imagine we'd have shared the double bed 'ben the room' during this period, but the practice of sharing bed space was so common throughout my boyhood, adolescence and early manhood that early sleeping arrangements rarely impinged on my consciousness.

What I am sure about are my grandfather's teaching methods. He is sitting bolt upright on a hard-backed kitchen chair with thighs outspread. Then this apple-cheeked bodach with the thick white hair, very like my own thatch today, and neatly trimmed white moustache beckons me forward, encircles my tiny waist with his large hands and lifts me bodily so that I stand between his legs, his face not ten inches away from mine. He has a soft face with smooth, pink skin. When he smiles, which he does often, his cheeks puff outwards. He has a lot of tiny lines running from the outside corners of his pale blue eyes. With his thumbs touching in the region of my belly and his other fingers laced together above my kidneys he gives me a gentle squeeze and invites me to join in with him as he sings his favourite Gaelic song, *A' Chruinneag Ìleach*, The Islay Maiden.

As the words pour out in languid gouts from his mouth I do not take my eyes off his mobile lip movements and, after trying to emulate them silently at first, eventually 'lift the melody' along with the old man whom I absolutely adore.

'*Ochoin, a Rìgh, gur e mi tha muladach*, Alas, Lord, it is I who am desolate,' we sing together. '*Nach robh mi 'n Ile 's mo rìbhinn lurach ann*, That I am not in Islay where my beautiful lover is, '*S i thogadh m' inntinn le brìodal cuireideach*, She would raise my spirits with her perfumed love-murmurings, '*S a chuir fo chìs mi mur' tìll i tuilleadh rium*, And will lay me low if she does not return to me.'

I can only guess at what these initial call and response sessions which old Iain favoured as preliminary warm-ups, followed by unison singing when I had mastered lyrics and melody, would convert to in man-hours. We may have been chanting, with breaks for strong, sweet tea, for up to four hours a day. Who's counting when you're having a good time?

'*An eilean uaine nan cluaintean glaiceagach*, It was in the green isle of the valleyed pastures, *A dh'fhàg mi 'ghruagach as uaisle cleachdaidhean*, That I left the maid of most noble demeanour: *Gur tric mi 'bruadar mo rùin bhith 'n taice rium*, Often I dream that my love is by my side, *Ach nuair nì mi dùsgadh mo rùin chan fhaicear leam*, But when I awake my love is not seen by me.'

At the age of four, I was a near-great Gaelic singer. My ear was okay; I was a gifted mimic. Unfortunately my voice was yet thin and I could hit a top note no louder or truer than most girls in my age bracket. The one preternatural gift I had was stamina. I could sing forever, and frequently did. I would repeat songs unimaginatively until people who shared lodgings with me begged me to stop.

While I suspect my cautious automatism might have made me a wee bit unpopular at times with my mother and father and the various people from the islands who came to visit, the one person who was a great fan was my maternal grandmother, *Anna Bheag nighean Aonghais 'ic Iain Mhòir*, who was from Old Mill, Griminish, Benbecula originally. After her husband Norman MacKinnon (*Tormod Ailein*) of *Cladach Baleshare*, North Uist was drowned in the North Sea while serving aboard the Royal Naval vessel the SS Holderness, she moved to a two-bedroomed flat in a red sandstone tenement in Midlock Street, Ibrox. This residence, though not all that distant from Brand Street, was definitely a step up in the housing chain. Later, when I returned to Glasgow from Uist, I learned to describe posh dwellings like this as being part of 'a building wi' a wally (tiled) close and bulgin' oot (bay) windaes.'

This was the scene of my greatest vocal triumph during my first sojourn in the city. I see the *cailleach*, broad of shoulder and beam, seated regally on an oversized chair. She is wearing a white linen apron upon which my gaze is fixed. I'm wearing a Maclean tartan kilt – I know this because I have before me a black and white photograph of me dated 1941 – scuffed shoes and a fawn Fair Isle jersey. Granny beckons. I lay my blond curls sideways on her apron which has deep side pockets. This action is not so much inspired by affection as by a desire to find out if she has a packet of sweets in her apron pocket. I hear the rustle of paper in my right ear.

I slyly look up to her swarthy face. *"Dè mar a chòrdadh ruibh òran math Gàidhlig a chluinntinn, a ghranaidh*, How would you like to hear a good Gaelic song, granny?"* I coo sweetly.

"Siuthad thusa, a ghràidhein, On you go, darling"* *Anna Bheag* replies, smiling fondly at her favourite grandchild.

(She once described my cousin Annie MacKinnon who was about my own age rather cruelly as a kind of alien. *"Saoilidh mi nach ann leam fhìn a tha i,* I don't think she's connected to me at all," was her dismissive opinion of poor Annie.)

"*Gabh thusa òran math Gàidhlig dhad sheanmhair,* You sing a good Gaelic song for your grandmother," she croons indulgently.

Near-concave chest inflated, fingernails digging into palms, I launch into my party piece. I finish, like my mentor, *Iain Eoghainn Ruaidh,* with a modest 'ral' and a hint of vibrato on the final '*riu-u-m.*'

Granny flips out. "Hurraa, Hurraa," she exclaims as she brings out the poke of caramels and extends it towards me.

At four years of age I was hooked: just a wee exhibitionist living imaginatively in the world described by the Roman poet Virgil in the 1st century AD and skipping without pause to the rejection endured by an unknown Islay bard in the nineteenth century.

TO BE ALIVE IS TO LEARN

It is a sunny Sunday afternoon in autumn. By this time I am a voracious consumer of the 'Yankee Comics', brightly coloured cartoon supplements brought home from the USA by my father, *Niall Mòr*. I've been allowed out into the 'back' and have become fluent in Govanese, though with my mother, *Peigi Bheag*, I prefer to converse in Gaelic. I am holding my mother's hand as we stroll along St Andrew's Drive in the leafy suburb of Dumbreck. My eye is caught by an enamelled street plaque, white lettering on a dark blue ground, which reads: ST ANDREW'S CIRCUS. "*Thugainn, a mhamaidh, suas dhan siorcas*, Come on, mammy, (let's go) up to the circus," I plead.

"No."

"Why not?"

"Because."

"*Ach tha mise airson na leoghainn 's na h-eich agus na 'clowns' fhaicinn*, But I want to see the lions and the horses and the clowns," I argue.

"*Uist, a ghlaoic ghrod tha thu ann*, Be quiet, you fool that you are," she explains. "It's not that kind of circus. All that's down that road are more and more big houses with big gardens, and the people who live there are certainly not clowns."

Small boy dissolves into sobbing tears. I'm consumed by a sense of unfairness. This is my first, but by no means my last, disappointment at the gap between anticipated pleasure and reality.

Another evening, again involving my mother, detaches itself from my archive of memories. I had heard from the youngsters in the back that The Shows were coming to the White City Dog Track about half a mile away on the Paisley Road West. The area between Helen Street and Broomloan Road is now taken up by the most secure police jail in Scotland.

During the war, at six-monthly intervals, groups of travelling carnival workers would mysteriously arrive on the site and erect their rides – the Waltzer, the Dodgem Car circuit, the sissy rocking horse merry-go-rounds – and the booths and kiosks inhabited by travellers as varied as Vince O'Hare, proprietor of an airgun shooting range, a fortune teller called Madam McCluskey, and a fat lady, her hair in curlers, who staffed the Toss-a-Penny-Onto-the-Plates booth. There were also various stands selling soft drinks and chips and fritters, details I remember because I managed to get my wee mother to take me to The Shows on no fewer than five evenings.

I always felt a sense of elation as we entered the magical domain of The Shows. I walked slowly in a tightly packed mass of people, all consuming vinegar and salt-drenched chips, round the perimeter of the showground. The entire area was a sonic mash of whistles and sirens, hurdy-gurdy music and amplified cackles. An American popular song about a Silver Dollar issued from the Kiddie Carousel. Human screams, difficult to distinguish from the recorded screams, added to the cacophony coming from the entrance to the Ghost Train. I was young and adored crowds, screams, and loud noises.

I dragged *Peigi Bheag* over to a riveting spectacle: Vince O'Hare's Cowboy Shooting Range. On a narrow counter five airgun rifles rested. Behind the counter stood Big Vince himself. He was six feet three, twenty-four years of age, and came from the Calton. He was wearing a ten-gallon hat, a Western shirt with piping on the chest and shoulders. It was his pants that fascinated me. They were red and had fringes running down each outer seam. He chain-smoked and grinned; he had an earring and a tattoo of a soaring eagle on the back of his hand. He looked at the passing punters like they were food. He picked up a microphone and recited the lines for his pitch: "Bring a stuffed animal home for a loved one": "Ye've goat tae knock the target doon tae win a bunny": "One shot, only a shilling": "Half a croon, three shots." Rows of stuffed animals were hanging by their feet above his head. He crooked a finger at me, beckoning me over to his booth.

I looked up at my mother.

She gave me a frozen stare and then shook her head from side to side twice, ve-ry slow-ly.

She tugged my hand and we resumed our walk round the fairground. The sight of Big Vince O'Hare, the be-fringed cowboy was emblazoned on my mind. If a cowboy had fringes down the sides of his pants and down the sleeves of his shirt – and he did – then I would have to have fringes too. Maybe people would think I was a cowboy. I'd be a hero in the 'back.' How would I get fringes? Make them myself. That would make me stand out.

So, okay, new plan. Get a pair of my mother's scissors. Then get to work.

Because I actually had a plan, I was pretty confident when I swiped the pinking shears from beside the sewing machine the following evening after Peigi had gone round the corner to a friend's house for a wee ceilidh.

I sat on the stairs leading up to the top landing and embarked on my career as a tailor or fashion designer. Carefully, without hurrying, tongue protruding from my mouth and eyes scrunched up in intense concentration, I made cuts one inch long in the hem of my light grey short trousers. When I squinted at my left thigh I was almost able to convince myself that at least one leg of my pants was decorated by a kind of fringe. I was intent on hacking at my right leg – a task that demanded a greater degree of concentration – and I didn't hear my mother coming up the stairs on her crepe-soled slip-ons until she was almost on top of me.

"*Bi cinnteach gum faigh do pheacdh a-mach thu*, Be sure that your sins will find you out." She wailed sorrowfully. "*Gu dè 'n truaighe a tha thu a' dèanamh le siosair*, What earthly use can you make of a pair of scissors?"

"*Nach seall sibh air na ribeagan a rinn mi air a' bhriogais agam, a mhàthair*, Won't you take a look at the fringe I've made on my trousers, mammy?" I said proudly.

"Why?" she asked in English, genuinely puzzled, I thought.

"I wanted to look like a cowboy," I replied, as though the answer was self-evident.

My mother mimed loading and firing a rifle. "*Tha thu cho gòrach ris na h-uiseagan*, you're as daft as the skylarks."

"How?"

"Cowboys didn't have fringes on trousers like yours."

"They didn't wear short trousers?"

"No, indeed."

"I didn't know that."

"*Fhad's a tha thu beò tha thu ag ionnsachadh, a Thormoid*, To be alive is to learn, Norman."

I placed the pinking shears on the step next to my ruined trousers and looked up at my mother's smiling face above me.

"*Chan e droch ghille a th' annad, a Thormoid*, direach rud beag foileach, You're not a bad boy, Norman, just a wee bit impetuous." She said as she rummaged in her handbag. "I have some coupons left, and I'm going to buy you "*Tofaidh na Bà*' with them." (McGowan's Highland Toffee had the image of a long-horned Highland Cow on the wrapper.)   She waved the book of sweetie coupons in front of me, fanning my solemn face with it.

"You worth it?" she said

I cocked my head, widened my eyes and grinned uncertainly.

"I don't know," *Peigi Bheag* said doubtfully. "You've ruined the trousers I made for you only last week."

I took her head between my little hands and whisper: "*Duilich*, Sorry"

She pressed her face forward until our cheeks were touching.

"I'm teasing you, Norman. Of course you're worth it."

We walked together to our outside door and went inside.

CHOCOLATES

It was on the last of these Show visits that I encountered a spectacle that has remained with me all my life. As we strolled along Paisley Road West we saw a crowd of maybe sixty people yelling and jostling in front of a café that stood next to a railway bridge on Broomloan Road.

Bellows and screams! Boo! … Aaaahh … Naaw! … Get right intae 'im! Then a chant began: "Chiperatatta no' ready – come back in five minutes!" … "Chiperatatta no' ready – come back in five minutes!" Out of this mass of angry people I could see fists in the air.

A muffled thud came from the front of the crowd. It could have been anything. I tugged my hand away from my mother's grasp and dived on all fours into the forest of legs, trousered and Lyle stockinged. I wriggled to the front of the semi-circle that surrounded the café. In the doorway two heavy set men in check sports jackets and flannels stood on either side of a skinny old man in a white apron and pulled the old man's arms away from the sides of his twitching body. The old boy was pleading in a foreign language. I cocked my head and let the torrent of Italian slip past me. My attention was now on a man of about thirty, stripped to the waist, who was standing in front of the plate glass window of the shop with his feet apart. He held in both his hands a long-handled hammer with a solid, heavy head. He swayed slightly from side to side and brought the hammer up to his shoulder. The onlookers, girls with bare arms raised aloft, youths with collarless shirts with sleeves rolled up to the elbows, middle aged women waving umbrellas, old men dragging deeply on cigarettes and pipes, all swayed from side to side in time to the shimmying of the man with the fourteen pound hammer.

Right! … Jist dae it, Jimmy! … Good on ye, son! … Gi'e 'im the message! Rumble, rumble, mutter booooo!

The head of the hammer struck the pane of glass with terrific force. The entire front window cascaded to the pavement.

Yegggh! …That's ma boy! …Go back tae Rome, ya bam! … Cheers, applause, jumping up and down.

One of the fat men released one of his hands and grabbed the little Italian's hair and pulled back on it. The skinny little man's head snapped back and he began to whimper. A short, stout woman wearing a headscarf over wiry grey hair slapped his cheeks repeatedly until he stopped. The fat man released his hair and the man's head dropped forward.

The bare-chested man stumbled through the space left by the smashed window. The crowd surged forward, glowering faces, snarling lips …then more shouts … Get the chocolates, Jimmy! … Throw the fags oot, Jimmy! … Chocolates! … Yegggghh!!

From the interior of the shop there flew boxes of chocolates, which burst open on contact with the pavement, spilling their contents at the feet of us in the front row. Packets of cigarettes, Capstan, Players, Gold Flake, Craven-A, followed in quick succession. The young girls, who were the most nimble and quick footed of the looters, scooped up the chocolate-coated fruit creams and truffles and offered them to everyone in the crowd.

Screams of delight and whoops of laughter! Yeggggghh! … munch, munch, munch, munch … Ya beauty!

One teenage girl with a twenty packet of Gold Flake tucked into the short sleeve of her blouse crunched through the broken glass and offered the box to me.

"Go on, son,"she said. "Help yirsel. Don't need coupons for this lot."

I fussily pawed through the scattered chocolates and gingerly picked up between forefinger and thumb a whirly creation that appeared undamaged and to be free of pavement dust. My lips were enclosing the confection when my arm was gripped and twisted downwards, forcing me to drop the sweet.

"*De mì-mhodh tha thu ris a-nis,* What carry on are you up to now?" my mother said.

"*Cha robh mi a' dèanamh dad,* I wasn't doing anything."

"*Bha thu an impis saoiteas ithe,* You were about to eat a sweetie."

"*Cha do leig sibh leam,* You didn't let me."

"*Cha do leig gu dearbh,* Indeed I did not!" *thuirt mo mhathair gu geur.*

"Carson, Why?"

"*Is e goid a rinn na blaigeartan air an Eadailteach,* These hooligans stole from the poor Italian."

"*De rud a chuir an cuthach orra,* What made them angry?"

"*Tha Mussolini is na h-Eadailtich a' gabhail leis na Gearmailtich anns a ' chogadh agus 's e siud a dh' fhag muinntir Ghlaschu cho fada an aghaidh ceannaichean Eadailteach anns a'bhaile seo,* Mussolini and the Italians have sided with the Germans in the war and that's what made the Glasgow folk resent the Italian shopkeepers in the city.

"*Chan fhaod mi rud milis fhaighinn, mar sin,* I can't get a sweetie, then?" I said.

"*Chan fhaod,* No,"my mother snapped. "*Mas e teoclaid a tha dhìth ort,* You want chocolate?" she said, her lips twisted in scorn. "*Thalla is iarr siud air tè Ghallda.* Ask any Lowland woman. *Cha bhi fhios aice siud gur e meirleach beag grod a th' annad,* She won't know that you're a rotten little thief."

MAMMY, WE WUZ ROBBED

I had been suffering pain in my throat for about ten days before my mother took me round to Dr Mitchell – that wasn't his birth name, I'm sure – and paid him two old shilling, or a florin, for the consultation. With a kindly manner he depressed my tongue and shone a light into my mouth.

"Badly inflamed, Mrs Maclean," he pronounces. He had a strong European accent, Viennese perhaps.

What shall we do?" my mother asks.

"Oh, they'll have to come out. Without (*vissout*) the shadow of a doubt."

"What will have to come out?" I croak in a weak voice.

"Your tonsils."

"How will you get them out?" I ask.

"Cut them."

I'm starting to suspect Dr Mitchell a bit. For someone in the business of healing people, he's making me feel considerably worse, and I have a strong impression, young as I am, that his clinical manner could do with a bit of work.

"You're going to cut something out of my throat?" I enquire.

"Not me. The surgeon in the hospital."

"Will it be painful?"

"Nein," Dr Mitchell chuckles. "Not painful ... well, maybe a wee bit. Surgeon does hundreds of these operations every year."

"Which hospital will he be going to?" my mother asks.

"Southern General."

"That's good," says my mother with relief in her voice. "We know one of the nurses there – Mairi Semnett."

Originally from the Point district of Lewis, Mairi had been undergoing nursing training in London when she had married a dashing young Frenchman the previous year. I haven't seen her since she announced her engagement to Pierre Simonet round at the Smiths' family home in Elizabeth Street. The pronunciation of the French surname in the mouth of our neighbour, Mrs. Smith — identified from early childhood as Cailleach 'Miff' — became 'Semnitt.' This sound I immediately associated with 'semmit' the Scottish word for a vest.

"You will have much fun there, Master Maclean," Dr Mitchell sighs. "In one day, operation the following morning. Then big surprise!"

"What?"

"They will of course knock you out before the cutting. When you wake up, the nurses will give you ... ice-cream!"

I had seen ice-cream cornets in the Yankee comics, but I'd never tasted any.

"Ah, ice-cream."

"Yes, you go to hospital ... little snip ... ice-cream, okay?"

"Okay."

"You a very brave little boy, Norman."

"Thank you."

"They are wunderbar in Southern General. You be strong little boy. And remember: ice-cream."

Just as my mother and I are leaving - the surgery is no more than a two bedroom flat, first right, low down, two blocks from the Smiths' house at the corner of Elizabeth Street and Brand Street – I turn at the door. The doctor inclines his head at me. He is not smiling.

A letter arrives at Brand Street from the southern General Hospital telling my mother she should report with me to a certain ward on a particular day. On our way down to Linthouse on the tram, my mother decides to stop off at Govan Cross. She takes me to a stationery shop in 'The Gollie.' There she buys me an 'Oor Wullie' annual. This is a gift, I now realise, to divert my attention from the long-anticipated ice-cream I can't stop frothing on about.

We duly arrive at the appointed place and I am led by a nurse to an assigned bed in a ward already occupied by three other boys. These lads seem to be in a really bad way. They lie on their backs with their noses protruding from crisp hospital sheets and are unresponsive to my cheery greetings. Oh-oh. Maybe I'm too well to have my tonsils cut from my throat. Yeah, maybe my mother and I have jumped the gun here. In a particularly inept attempt to fit in, I decide to prattle in Govanese. "Hey," I shout, "do you guys know that after they take our tonsils out we're getting heaps of ice-cream?"

"No' me," says the pale faced boy in the bed opposite mine.

"Oh, aye," I reply confidently. "Everybody gets ice-cream after the operation. It's a rule. It's to soothe the pain afterwards."

"But I'm no' in for my tonsils."

"What are you in for, then?"

"I'm in to get cut, but no' in my throat."

"Where?"

"You know …" He stammers in embarrassment. "They're … they're going to cut me somewhere else. Like … you know … er, down below."

"Is that true, aboot the ice-cream?" says another of the boys from the prone position. Before I can reassure him, a deeper, more gravelly voice interrupts.

"Listen," this third lad interjects. "See, if you're makin' a' this up aboot the ice-cream, somebody'll hiv tae explain tae ye how things work. Ye don't want me tae hiv tae gi'e ye the 'malky', dae ye?" He raises his head from the pillow and looks directly at me, eyes narrowed but unblinking. I notice he's quite old, at least eleven or twelve, and while I don't understand what the 'malky' means, I do appreciate the threat of physical violence that lies beneath the word.

"Stand on me, pal," I say, with appreciably less confidence than before. "You'll get yir ice-cream. Nae bother. Honest. Dr Mitchell told me, and so did the Miffs, Miff hersel' and her three daughters, Ina, Betty and Ann."

"Ye're gibberin' noo, ya wee nyaff."

"Naw, straight up, Jimmy. It's true."

"It'd better be. Or else you'll be hearin' fae me."

I crash on my narrow bed with the sheet and blanket draped over my head and when I wake the same nurse comes in with a cart. On it there are various stainless steel dishes and a machine sprouting wires with sticky tabs attached to them. She places the tabs all over my body and picks up a tiny syringe from one of the steel dishes. She plunges the tip of the needle into the back of my hand. Nothing hurts. I want to set up house with this angel. I'm not even six yet. I lie doing nothing for about half a minute, then feel myself heading for the good, relaxing sleep.

When I come round, it is like I've slept for three days and all I am aware of is that my throat feels slightly raw and there is a metallic taste in my mouth.

"So, when am I getting it?" I ask the wee, round nurse with the white handkerchief on her dark, tight curls who is hauling me into an upright position.

"Getting what?"

"Och, come on, miss. You know what I'm talking about."

"No, I don't, son."

"The ice-cream," I blurt out. Even saying the word makes my saliva flow.

"What ice-cream, Norman?"

Is she teasing me? I check out her eyes. Nope. She doesn't know about the ice-cream.

"Where are the rest of the boys?" I ask.

"Still in the operating theatre."

Oh, that's it. They're waiting until all four of us recover –well, maybe not the lad who's getting cut 'down below' – until the three of us who are getting our tonsils out, including that tough guy from the Wine Alley, come round.

"What were you expecting, dear?" the wee, round nurse enquires.

I make an indecipherable whining noise. I clear my throat which causes a sharp pain to shoot from the site of my missing tonsils.

"You know, I really, um ..." I'm worried that she thinks she's failed me in some way, so I say: "I think I should talk with your boss, because she obviously hasn't told you about the special treat we're due."

"All right," she sighs. "I'll go and get Sister to talk to you."

"Thank you," I whisper insincerely. "That will be good."

"Back in five minutes," she says, waddling away from my bedside and making for the door.

"Norman! Hey, wee man! What can I do for you?"

I seem to have fallen asleep. The head nurse is a white-haired little old lady with spectacles.

"Hello. I need ... um, I need my ice-cream now."

"What ice-cream?"

"The stuff I was promised."

"Who promised you?"

"I just ... didn't ... I mean, Dr Mitchell, everybody at the Miffs ... everybody."

"You might not want to listen to people outside." I notice her tone has become somewhat sharp.

"Why not?"

She gives me a frozen smile that says I don't know how the world works. "This is a hospital, Master Maclean. It is not a place to be eating ice-cream. Ice-cream is wonderful, but this place is about getting you better. Do you understand?"

"But ..." I fidget. "I know people in this hospital – very important people – and they won't like it if I'm forced to complain about you."

"So, what are you going to do?"

"I'm going to tell my friend who works here that you're refusing to give me the ice-cream you owe me."

"What's your friend's name?"

"I call her 'Almost-a-doctor'."

"What's her real name?"

Bad question, Sister. I can't remember.

"I forget."

"A-ha. You forget?"

"No, wait – it'll come back to me."

"Hurry up. I have other patients to see. What is the name of your friend who is, in your own words, 'almost a doctor'?'

"Her married name has to do with clothing."

Like ... 'coat' or 'pants' or something like that?"

Faint pulse.

"Uh ... it's more like underclothes."

"Go on, please."

"She's married to a Frenchman."

"Is it 'Vesté' do you think?"

Stronger pulse.

"It's on the tip of my tongue ... it's ... Got it! She's called ..." I spit out the words triumphantly, "Nurse Drawers!"

I have a rough idea why I said such a thing: 'Simonet'

sounding in old Mrs Smith's 'Mau' accent like 'Semnitt' and this being heard by me as 'Semmit', the Scottish term for vest. It's a short leap from vest to underpants or drathais, drawers. It just sort of appeared like an aura, then came out like a seizure.

The Sister's thin lips part in what passes as a smile. Boom! I hardly know how to recover. Above the thick, square framed spectacles, the Sister's brows have bent into bat wings and I am acutely aware that I've said something stupid. The only way out of it, I think, is to start laughing and pretend I'm such a merry wag that I've uttered these silly words in a spirit of pranksterism and joy. I am laughing uncontrollably and in the process of turning my back on the sole witness to my stupidity. I lose in my attempt to hide when the Sister says, "Norman?"

I turn to face her.

"Let me explain something to you," she says primly. "It is not hospital policy to serve ice-cream … ever."

"You mean I'm probably not going to be eating ice-cream for … like … a while. Like … ever, maybe?"

"Not in the immediate future," she answers curtly. "Now, get up and get dressed. Your mum's coming to collect you in half an hour."

I spend the following thirty minutes sitting, fully booted and spurred, in a crouch on the edge of my narrow bed casting anxious glances at the swing doors. First to make a horizontal entry on a gurney was a lad about my own age who brightened up when he regained consciousness and saw me sitting there.

"Hi-ya," he croaks. "Have you had the ice-cream yet?"

"No."

"That's good."

"No, that's bad."

"How?"

"You're not going to get any ice-cream."

"But … but, you said it was a law."

"Well, it is … kind of."

"What happened?"

"They broke the law."

"That's no' fair."

"You're going to get a 'doin' fae that big boy."

"Too late," I crow triumphantly as I catch sight of my wee mother bumping her way through the swing doors, message bags draped over both forearms. "I'll leave you to explain to him why the ice-cream has been discontinued. As for the other boy …"

I pause.

Don't go there, *a Thormoid*.

"… don't bother about him. He wasn't due ice-cream anyway."

"*De bha gur cumail*, What kept you?" I scream hysterically at my mother as I hop off the bed and grab the 'Oor Wullie' annua.

"*An robh thu a' gabhail fadachd, a ghraidh*, Did you feel the time long, dear? My mother says.

I say nothing and hustle her and me out of the accursed place at speed.

PHILATELY

On a Monday morning in September, Miss Condie, teacher of the infant class at Bellahouston Primary, sits, pen in hand, at an upright desk in front of a class of five-year-olds. She is tall and trim with short, thick hair, going from brown to grey.

"Now, children," she coos, "I want each of you to come out and give me the pennies you got from your parents this morning when I call your name."

This is the preliminary call of a ritual known as the 'Milk Money Handover.' The way the deal works is like this: one little, squat bottle of milk containing the third of a pint is given to each pupil throughout the school after the morning break. The price for a week's supply is tuppence halfpenny.

I have been a participant in this ritual for barely six weeks and, as I sit at a desk in the front row of the classroom, I've got the drill off pat. I dutifully quickstep up to the desk when she calls my name.

"Thank you, Norman," Miss Condie says with a lilt in her voice after I hand over the money and she makes a mark in an open ledger. "And how are you settling down here at school? Do you like coming here every day?"

"Very much, Miss," I reply. "But I don't know if I'll be coming here much longer."

"Why not?"

"It's the air-raids every night, Miss."

"The school's only open during the day, Norman. At night we're all safely tucked up at home, or, if there's a German bombing raid, we go with our neighbours to our air-raid shelters, don't we, dear?"

"But ..."

"Oh, I know you think I sleep in the cupboard behind me ..." She pauses and some of the class snigger at the absurdity of the proposition ..."but I can assure you, Norman, that when the janitor rings the bell at three o'clock I go home to my house, just as you do."

"No, Miss," I protest. "I don't think you sleep in the cupboard." This is indeed contrary to the opinion of the lad who shares the double desk with me, Ally Bell, an undersized boy who has an attention span far smaller than that of most of the class and who struggles with the two-times table. "I know," I continue, "you go home at three. It's just..."

"Just what, Norman?"

"It's my father."

"What about him?"

"He's home on leave from the Merchant Navy just now and he's worried about my mother and me being safe here in Glasgow."

"But what can we do about the attacks the Luftwaffe are making on Clydeside?"

"He's thinking of sending my mum and me up to the Highlands ... to my granduncle at the head of Loch Arkaig."

"Tell him not to worry. It's getting safer all the time here in the city. You're doing very well here in your first month at school. Your reading and counting skills are excellent, and we wouldn't want to lose you." She turns her head to appeal to my classmates. "We don't want to lose Norman, do we, class?"

There comes a resounding chorus in unison of 'no, Miss' and I am thrilled to see that Dorothy McWee, the poster girl of our cohort, is among the most enthusiastic of those who don't want me to leave for the north. She is smiling broadly and fluttering her eyelashes while smoothing the fringe from her brow. This I interpret as a silent affirmation of how wonderful I am. I am greatly pleased and immediately decide to become her special boyfriend.

Dorothy stands no more than three and a half feet off the ground and her strawberry blond hair is so straight it doesn't even curl at her shoulders – it just slides by. She's just so cute. The way she holds her face, it's like she always knows the best angles. Unfortunately, she is the spoiled only child of middle-class parents (her dad works in an office 'up the town' and her mum is a nursing sister in the Elder Cottage Hospital) who own a detached villa in leafy Dumbreck.

At play-time, I waste no time in approaching her.

"Heyyyy," I call as I approach her with my right arm thrust forward.

"Hi-ya," she replies and tickles my open palm with the tips of her fingers.

"Norman," I say.

"I know who you are," she replies. "Are you really going to leave our school?"

"Maybe."

"Do you want to be my boyfriend?"

"Yes, yes, you look gorgeous."

"And that's why you want to be my boyfriend?"

"I …" I can't think up an answer quickly enough. "I just want to look at you all the time. You know …if I become your boyfriend

I'll be able to look at you all I want in school. That will make me really happy."

"Okay," she says, "this is a bit embarrassing, but I wouldn't mind being your girlfriend for a bit. I heard about how you speak a different language in your home. And I always thought you were cute but I always thought you were so shy that you wouldn't be fun to be pally with. I didn't realize that you were like, different. And I think that's smashing and maybe I'll be your girlfriend."

Here is a girl who can help me to become like everybody else.

"So, we're boyfriend and girlfriend now, are we?" I ask.

"Just about," she replies, "but you'll have to give me a present before we tell other folk."

"What?"

"You've got to give me something nice I can tell mummy and daddy a boy in my class gave me."

So it's like that, I think.

"Don't you want to get invited over to my house to have cake and lemonade on Saturday afternoon?"

I nod enthusiastically. I am filled with that crazy seeing-someone-else's house energy. I perform a little jig as the bell sounds for resumption of classes. I'm in Primary One and I have a girlfriend. This is me, set for life.

I have, however, a major problem. I am, as the Weegies say 'Borassic Lint' –skint, broke, tapped out. I've no way of getting 'something nice' for Dorothy. Maybe I can find something in our house that will please her. But I know that's a non-starter.

Hold it, Norrie! The wee paper shop at the corner of Midlock Street and Paisley Road West, opposite the school gates, has foreign stamps in polythene envelopes. Hoooooooo-ee!

"How much are the foreign stamps?" I ask the old man in the shop at exactly three minutes past three.

45

"Tuppence furr a packet o' four: a tanner (sixpence) furr the big packet wi' fifteen stamps in it," the old man growls.

"Look, keep one of the wee packets – the stamps with the birds on them – for me, will you?" I ask.

"How long?"

"A week today."

"A'right."

For the rest of the week in class I gaze at Dorothy from afar. I look eager and stupid.

She responds by wiggling her fingers at me and flicking her hair behind her ear. That's nearly a kiss, I imagine. If I had given her the brightly coloured foreign stamps that would be a kiss.

Next Monday morning, at exactly five minutes to nine I hand over two pennies to the old man in the paper shop and receive three rectangular and one triangular postage stamps purporting to be from Asuncion, Mauritius, Trinidad and Tobago and, I think, Hungary. They are objects of beauty – attractive images in bright colours of exotic birds and muscled warriors – and Dorothy will love them.

You, Norman, learn to show love to your mother, hug your dad, come first in the class, touch Dorothy, hold her hand, run in the park with her, go for a picnic with her, learn how to swim, dance, and run free.

I think I tell Miss Condie at the 'Milk Money Handover' that my mother hasn't given me any money and that I don't like milk anyway. I wait impatiently for the morning interval.

"Dorothy," I announce in the playground, "I have something for you." I hand over the little envelope.

She looks at it and gasps. "What's this?"

"Foreign stamps."

"You're giving me foreign stamps as a present?" She is staring at me in disbelief.

"No, no, um …just the first of many presents."

46

She pulls her hair back from her face with both hands, holding it there, eyes wide and angry. The present is dropped on the dimpled concrete slabs of the playground and the last I ever see of Dorothy McWee is a glimpse of her spindly legs walking away from her philatelic suitor.

I decide to head home, and five years are to pass before I enter these school gates again. I am not in any hurry to get to 191 Brand Street and I dally in the American Swing Park one block away from our tenement. This is a bad way to pass the time until the end of the school day.

I don't think that, of course, my absence from class will have been reported to the Truant Officer and that Miss Condie will have been told of the expenditure of my milk money on foreign stamps. The weird thing is that I do not step immediately into the kitchen of our house. I stop in the lobby and call my mother's name twice. She wails in reply. Big Neil steps from behind the bathroom door, shows me the leather razor strop he holds between clenched fists and tells me to go before him into the kitchen where I see my mother sitting on the bed leaning forward with her head between her palms.

My father looms over me. I stare at him in mute defiance.

No, I didn't give the money to Miss Condie … Yes, I gave it to the man in the paper shop … Postage stamps from foreign countries … Pictures of birds with brightly coloured plumage … Beautiful … No, I'll not tell you who they were for … No, I didn't steal the milk money … No … No … No …

Big Neil snaps the leather belt before my tearful eyes. The leather is brown with blackish stains throughout its length – like a malevolent snake – and as he orders me to strip I begin to whimper.

BUNDLE AND GO

The single-track road on the north shore of Loch Arkaig meandered westward towards Srathan where my mother and I were to spend about a year and a half with the family of my granduncle, *Seumas Mòr mac Aonghais 'ic Iain Mhòir*, James Macdonald, or Big Jimmy, son of Angus, son of Big John. Prompted by fear of Hitler's bombs, the government and parents motivated by self-help, initiated a programme of re-location for thousands of children from all over Britain. Kids like me were being transferred from the great cities of the UK to safer locations in the countryside. We were known as 'evacuees', which I thought a romantic term. Not that I was on any official government scheme: kids of Irish descent in Glasgow were sent to grandparents in Donegal, and young Glasgow Gaels made for ancestral homes all over the West Highlands and Islands.

In 1941 a Luftwaffe pilot aiming to cripple the Clyde shipyards released a bomb which landed in the middle of Blackburn Street in the Plantation district of Govan. The site of the explosion which left a crater about thirty feet wide and maybe twenty feet deep in the cobbled street was visited by my father and me on a winter morning. I clearly remember standing with a mittened hand enclosed by my dad's big fist looking wide eyed at the destruction. *"An deachaidh duine a ghoirteachadh*, Was anybody hurt?" I asked. *"Cha deach' an turas seo*, Not this time," was the cryptic reply. I do believe this was the stimulus for *Niall Mòr* sending me and *Peigi Bheag* up to her uncle's home in remote Lochaber.

A little vignette featuring father and very young son asserts itself unbidden. I had just been accused, unjustly I thought, of stealing my weekly milk money and had endured a savage beating from this same father. I had convinced myself that after going up against the razor strop, I didn't have to fear this man anymore and I was invincible. With regard to Big Neil's disproportionate response to my buying foreign stamps I entertained the suggestion that he wanted to perpetrate a cruel deed because he felt guilty about something he had done in the past. The manifold subtleties of these psychological gems, mine and daddy's, might test a hardened psychiatrist.

I accompany Big Neil on a trip to Bobby Crawford's newspaper shop in Ibrox Street. There, my father purchases the Citizen newspaper, a packet of ten Capstan cigarettes, 'sticks' – pre-packed bundles of firewood that my mother used as kindling before banking the kitchen fireplace with coal from the bunker in the 'lobby' or hallway. – and a final item, which my dad allows me to choose: a bottle of 'ginger'. My preference is for American Cream Soda.

We have turned the corner into Elizabeth Street and are approaching the junction with Middleton Street when my father directs my attention towards a lamppost at the corner of the pavement. This is a metal fluted column, tapering from a base of around ten inches in diameter to six inches or so at the point where a rectangular iron crossbar extended for ten inches on either side of the vertical column. Weirdly enough, I remember that I make a definite effort to memorise the embossed Roman letters on this horizontal appendage. They are, reading from left to right: G.C., this on the left arm, and L.D. on the right. (Much later I learned that this was an acronym for Glasgow Corporation Lighting Department.)

Perched above the iron supports is a diamond shaped globe made up of sixteen rectangular panes of glass, measuring maybe six by ten inches. The eight upper windows are separated from the lower panes at an angle of forty-five degrees. Within this lantern shape was a white mantle attached to an S-shaped brass coil which emerges from the steel column. Access to the lantern is achieved by way of a kind of metal trap door at its base. We, the members of our wee gang in the late forties, often shinnied our way up to the logo-bearing crossbars, but we have never succeeded in opening up this trap door.

No, the only man able to do that is the 'Leerie' or Lamplighter. It is clear that in an era when streets and closes are gas lit somebody has to turn the gas on and off. The chosen one to perform these essential tasks is known as the 'Leerie.' An ironic folk song of the period celebrates his ubiquity and industry.

> When the shades of night are falling,
> Comes a figure everyone knows:
> It's 'Auld Wullie, the Leerie'
> Spreading light wherever he goes.

His only piece of apparatus is his pole. This is a slim mahogany or ebony baton around six feet in length and about four inches in diameter. At the business end there are gleaming brass ferules from which sprout mysterious brass hooks and key-shaped protuberances. This is the old wizard's magic wand. At the very top of the implement there protrudes a slim curved worm of brass which contained what I think of as an eternal flame. After jemmying open the metal trap door by inserting one of the hooks into the edge of the metal he twists and taps various keys in the interior. Finally, he inserts his 'eternal flame' into the lantern and ignites the gas-filled mantle. A few more fiddly adjustments to the controls inside terminates with the faint crash of the metal trap door as, with a slight twist of his wrists, he seals off the lantern until dawn the next day. The entire operation takes less than two seconds and he then shoulders his 'pole' and continues on his plodding way to the nearest close to bring light to the tenement dwellers within.

Of course, what I didn't know for a long time was that the tiny peep of flame that issued from the brass swan-neck worm at the end of his pole was not an 'eternal' flame. It was fuelled by a substance everybody called 'carbide.' When the old 'Leerie' was made aware that his fuel was running low, he would perform a mysterious ritual at the kerbside, always ensuring that he was in the vicinity of a ribbed grate or 'stank.' First of all, he'd unscrew the brass ferule at the end of the pole. Then, very gingerly, he'd upend the baton and, with the kind of excessive care of a forensic scientist or a UN weapons inspector, he'd gently tap the contents of the cylinder into the drain.

While 'Auld Wullie' had undoubtedly the hand-eye co-ordination of a professional golfer or tennis player when performing the footery little tasks associated with lighting the gas lamps, it was undeniable that when it came to disposing the detritus of the 'carbide' or whatever chemical substance was contained in the body of his pole he wasn't always fastidious. Frequently, not all the residue went down the drain, and there would be little pyramids of white powder left near the ribbed 'stank.'

It is to such a little pile of powder that Big Neil directs my attention that day as we return home with our errands.

"*Seall air seo, a Thormoid*, Look at this, Norman," he commanded.

"*Dè th' ann*, What is it?"

"*Sgudal a' bhodaich*, The old man's rubbish," he announces curtly as he opens the bottle of American Cream Soda and pours a glassful of the stuff on to the little mound of white powder.

Miraculously, there occurs a violent flaring up of the compound, the original powder fizzing up to three times its original size accompanied by a hissing sound and minute particles sparking into the air. *Chan fhaca mi a leithid eadar mo dhà shùil riamh*, I've never seen the likes of this ever in my entire life.

"*Leis na ìnnleachdan a th' aig na Gearmailtich dh'fhaodadh iad sgrios mar sin a dhèanamh air Brand Street*, With the armament the Germans possess they could inflict the same damage on Brand Street."

"*O, athair, na bithibh a' bruidhinn mar sin*, Oh, dad, don't talk like that.

"*Ma thilgeas iad boma air an togalach againne, bidh guthan, agus tàirneanaich, agus dealanaich, agus crith-thalmhainn ann*, If they throw a bomb on our tenement, there will be noises, thunderings, lightning, and an earthquake."

I am silent as we leave the bubbling mass next to the lamp post and walk slowly back home. I am convinced that my father is seriously considering the removal of me and my mother from the danger zone of the city.

It was the gas mask that finally decided him. In September 1941, Johnny Bankhead, who was a pupil in a class or two above mine in Bellahouston Primary School and who lived with his mother, father and young brother Andy across the landing from us, was issued with a gas mask. It came in a cardboard box, very like a binocular case with straps. Johnny brought the evil smelling gadget out on to the landing and Andy and I had a great time scaring each other by pretending to issue commands in German. I think I was bellowing 'Achtung! Hilfe! Achtung!' and I was thrilled by the metallic timbre of my voice as it emerged from the tin grill at the base of the hideous rubber snout of this weird piece of apparatus. It was at that moment that *Niall Mòr* mounted the twelve steps that led to our landing. Without a word he whipped the mask off my face and threw it at Johnny. The Bankhead brothers retreated rapidly to their own home. With a firm grip on the back of my neck Big Neil marched me into the kitchen of our house where my mother was standing at the cooker.

"That's it, Peggy," he announced firmly in English. "Please sit down for a minute and I'll tell you what you're going to do." This was heavy. Whatever he was about to say was rendered extremely important in my mind by his employment of English as his mode of expression.

"What's this about?" my mother asked, accepting that this was no idle hearth-side exchange.

"*Srathan*," my father snapped.

"And?"

"You and the boy are going there next Monday," my father announced firmly.

"Now's the time, Peggy. You'll go up to Queen Street Station tomorrow and buy two tickets to Spean Bridge. As you know, I'm going back to sea on Friday, but before I ship out I'll send a telegram to your uncle asking him to arrange a lift with Donnie the Post up the glen to Srathan."

"But, Neil ..." my mother began to protest but was cut off by her husband.

"There's no 'but' in it," my father said brusquely. "The pair of you are off to *Seumas Mòr's* next Monday. I'll order Frank Ottolini's taxi to pick you up at quarter past five that morning. You'll get the five-fifty Mallaig train, and Donnie MacLachlan the Postie will meet you at Spean at ten." With that he turned on his heel and left my mother and me speechless as he headed for the outside door. Over his shoulder he shouted: "*Tha mi a' dol sìos gu Howden's feuch am beir mi air pinnt,* I'm going down to Howden's to see if I can grab a pint." He rushed out.

My mother and I sit open-mouthed at the kitchen table and I felt an abyss of panic open beneath me.

THE MALLAIG TRAIN

A memory inside me is trying to wrestle its way through to consciousness. In my mind there is a vaguely sketched railway compartment, sliding door leading to an interior corridor, two facing bench seats with overhead racks, and a window dark with coal dust overlooking bleak Rannoch Moor just north of Loch Tulla. I am occupying the full extent of the banquette nearer the locomotive, and as I stretch out on my right side I gaze at my mother in the corner opposite me and a soberly-dressed gentleman seated at the corner near the door. He has wispy black hair that straggles about his head as if it is lost. I am unable to guess his age, but I conclude he must be about the same age as my mother's youngest brother, Cailean Beag, Wee Colin: that is, around thirty. At the time of our flight from the city my uncle Colin had been serving as an infantryman with the Cameronians since the outbreak of WWII. He was a vivid presence in my life since he spent any leaves between his mother's house in Ibrox and our home in Brand Street.

"Are you a minister?" my mother asks the man, indicating the white linen band peeping above the collar of his black blouse.

"No, I'm a priest," the smiling man replies. "Father Michael, lately of Bellshill, Lanarkshire." He extends an arm to shake my mother's hand. "And who's this?" he adds, nodding affectionately in my direction.

"This is my son, Norman," my mother says.

"Is that the Gaelic I heard you talking earlier?"

"Yes. We speak Gaelic at home."

Here it comes –same response this information always provokes among monoglot English speakers.

"You weren't talking about me, were you?" the priest says hopefully, half-kidding, wholly earnest.

"Of course not," my mother assures him.

"And can Norman understand English?"

"Oh, yes," Peigi announces, barely concealing the pride in her voice. "He can read and write it as well …and he's just started school."

"Bright kid," he says with genuine admiration. "What are you going to be when you grow up, Norman?"

"A shepherd."

"A shepherd?"

"Och, don't listen to him," my mother interrupts. "Ever since he was told that we were going to Loch Arkaig to my uncle's sheep farm he's talked about nothing but sheep and lambs."

"Where do you get off the train to get to this … er, Loch Arkaig?"

"Spean Bridge."

"Same here," Father Michael offers.

"Will they have sheep in Spean Bridge?" I enquire, displaying the enthusiasm for a newfound passion that I'm afraid has dogged me all my life.

"No, Norman, I'm not staying in Spean. I'm going on to the Abbey at Fort Augustus."

"Is that business or pleasure?" my mother says.

"Neither," the priest answers. "I'm going to the Abbey to dry out."

"But you're not even damp," I protest.

"No," the priest laughingly explains. "They're offering me rehabilitation at the Abbey.

"Why do you need rehabilitation? Were you in the war?" my mother asks.

"In a way, I was in a war, and I was definitely losing."

"What do you mean?" my mother asks.

"I was drinking myself to death."

All three of us fall silent.

We arrive at Spean Bridge railway station around ten in the morning. Donnie the Post's wee red van is parked in the station courtyard.

"Have you got a lift?" *Peigi Bheag* asks Father Michael.

"Yes, the taxi's down the road beside the hotel," he says, pointing down the driveway.

"You sure?"

The priest looks sad. Shaking his head he takes. a packet of cigarettes from his jacket pocket and says good-bye. "Tend your flock well, Norman," he calls out.

As my mother and I clamber into Donnie the Post's van, I look back and see Father Michael wipe his eyes with the back of his hand.

THE LAND OF LOCHIEL

The little narrow road on the north shore of Loch Arkaig curls around bays and rocky promontories and plunges over hills and gullies as it meanders westward towards *Srathan* where my mother and I are to spend about a year and a half with the family of my granduncle, *Seumas Mòr mac Aonghais 'ic Iain Mhòir*, James Macdonald, or Big Jimmy, son of Angus, son of Big John. *Seumas Mòr* and his wife *Màiri* (née Patterson, from one of the few Protestant families in Daliburgh, South Uist) and their children, Kenny, Annie, Bella, Nan, Murdo and Christopher, all showed great kindness to my mother and me during the last three years of the Second World War.

From one world to another I fly at great speed like the shuttle on my grandmother's loom. I've moved from an English-speaking environment into an exclusively Gaelic-speaking one. There is in the kitchen in Srathan an inordinate emphasis on oral fluency. When I recall the deliveries of my mentors, *Seumas Mòr* himself and a visiting shepherd from Skye called *Coinneach* 'Tin', I am struck by the similarities in styles. They and famous raconteurs in Benbecula later on favoured a kind of epic mode of delivery. All of them, whether narrating a pre-Christian folk tale or throwing out the latest scandal overheard in the Post Office or pub, contained more than a hint of performance in their delivery. Dialogue between protagonists was faithfully reproduced. Suspense was beautifully protected over the nature of the horrific or hilarious event that was about to take place. It is little wonder that I gravitated towards showing off.

When I was five I joined Bella, Nan, Murdo and Christopher — and two Robertson brothers, whose father, a Skyeman, was the shepherd in Kinlocharkaig — in the little corrugated-iron schoolhouse that stood on the main road three hundred yards up the hill, to be taught the alphabet by a spinster called Miss MacLean. However, there is no doubt that, outside the classroom, my prosbaig or telescope was trained on the vertical Gaelic plane during the years I spent in Lochaber and Benbecula. Later on, in my so-called higher education, it would waver on the horizontal plane, thus laying the foundation for the cultural schizophrenia that I suffered for most of my life.

I received a premonition of this conflict one stormy night in Strathan. As Christopher and I lay snugly in bed covered by heaps of blankets, listening to the merciless rain rattling against the windows, we became aware that visitors had arrived at the house. Muffled voices, shuffling feet and unidentifiable noises downstairs drew us on tiptoe to the living room, where a strange sight greeted our eyes. The room was full of soldiers, maybe a dozen of them, in drenched khaki uniforms covered by ponchos. They were carrying rifles, haversacks and rucksacks that they were divesting themselves off as we watched from the doorway. The flashes on their shoulders proclaimed POLSKA, and the sibilant language they spoke in declared that they came from Eastern Europe. Later I found out that they were trainee commandos from Spean Bridge who had set off on a night exercise, got hopelessly lost in the mist and rain, and had sought shelter from *Seumas*. How the old man had understood the request was a mystery. The Polish captain commanded only limited English and Seumas had next to none. Doubtless the vodka on the dresser made communication a little easier. Our patriarch said they could sleep in the hay shed, but it was early yet and it would be churlish of him to refuse the gifts his grateful visitors had brought him. The night passed in wild carouse of drinking and music and, not only were the wee interlopers allowed to remain up, but they too were the recipients of gifts from the soldiers. Thick slabs of dark chocolate were taken from emergency ration tins and piled into our laps. As I listened to a young Pole sing to the delight of the Macdonald ladies, there was the sense that everything that was going on was right. The total unexpectedness of the faint revelation that followed set my mind in turmoil. The curvature of the earth, I told myself, promised new people and experiences just beyond the horizon.

Night after night, during the final quarter of the year I spent in the glen, our house was full of people who used to come air chèilidh, visiting. Along with members of the Macdonald clan, there would always be two or three unmarried shepherds, a gamekeeper from Glendessary and a quartet of woodcutters from Achnacarry. With the sour smell of damp wool steadily growing stronger we would find a place to sit as best we could in the glow of the hissing Tilley lamp, which stood on the kitchen table. *Crìstean*, Christopher, the youngest of the Macdonald family, and I would crouch on the linoleum on the floor with our arms around our knees, and more often than not there would be a pair of retired collie dogs between us. My grand-uncle always lolled in the big armchair beside the black 'American' stove, his big piper's hand tightly gripping a mug of strong tea that was constantly topped up by his wife, *Màiri*, or by his daughters, Anabella and Nan. Another daughter, *Annag* or Annie, the eldest member of the family now that Kenny had left home, had contracted tuberculosis in Austria while serving in the WRAC, and was not allowed to do anything in the house. My mother, her sister's daughter, always tuned the needle of the radio to somewhere between Hilversum and Prague so that we could hear the news bulletins, and I suspect that she and *Annag* were the only ones in the room who fully understood the English language of the newsreader.

Certainly, the two youngest sons, *Murchadh* and *Crìstean*, and I did not gather from the clipped gibberish that whined out of the box that the war was coming to an end. Christopher and I would be making preparation for the entertainment to follow.

We would bring out the violin and the practice chanter, a battered old set of Glen bagpipes and a wheezy button-key melodeon with two spoons on the bass end that could only produce hoarse farmyard noises. Annag and some of the lads would descend on the instruments as soon as the broadcast ended and the old man turned off the radio. Very soon, loping jigs and fast, lively reels would be heard, to the accompaniment of much hand clapping and stamping of feet. The adults who were not playing instruments formed partners and with crossed hands swung in cirlces on the spot, and Seumas Mòr himself would get up, raise his arms aloft and perform rapid heel-toe shuffles in the centre of the room. When they tired of the dancing everyone took a turn at singing, playing or telling a story. My mother would sing a song about a young girl married to an old man whom she did not love. *Horo chan eil cadal orm*, Horo I am not sleepy, was the first line of it, and as the words swelled in her mouth I could taste some of the great longing that was eating away at her.

FALSE FINGERING

It was on the island of Benbecula that I spent the second stage of my exile from the Big Smoke.

On the whole, I integrated fairly well into the island community. Although the Gaelic language provided a mutual frame of reference between the locals and myself, on one occasion I felt my heart plummet towards my 'wellies' as shame washed over me.

The sun is setting as a herd of a dozen or so boys and girls, all under the age of twelve, file into the staff-room for the auditions with *Donnchadh Ruairidh Dhonnchaidh*, Duncan MacLellan, from Caolas Fhloddaidh, Kyles Flodda, who was the piping instructor on the island of Benbecula. His classes were held on Wednesdays at the close of the normal school day at *Sgoil Chnoc na Mòna* or Torlum Public School. Each member of our mini-platoon of hopefuls clutches a practice chanter and an alarmingly large number of our cohort has a copy of Logan's Bagpipe Tutor tucked under armpits. Until this moment I've had no idea that such a publication existed. Indeed, I'm not even aware there is an agreed way to play the Great Highland Bagpipe. My cousins, *Murdoch* and *Crìstean*, and I had learned a very small part of a rudimentary version of a Gaelic love song whose first line was *Ho-ro, mo nighean donn bhoidheach*, My brown-haired maiden. Without formal instruction from a journeyman piper, we had essentially taught ourselves to replicate, approximately, the melody of the song.

We rookies, the primary school pupils who are keen on becoming pipers, have to stand with our backs to the three walls of the room while we wait for the senior pupils to finish their practice. What I am hearing is to my untutored ears little short of miraculous. About ten boys and perhaps four girls are belting out on their practice chanters the fourth part of a Jig which I recognise from extended sessions listening to the Mulcahey Brothers and other Irish Ceili Bands on Radio Athlone as a tune called The Rakes of Kildare. What blows me sideways is that while two thirds of the group are playing in unison another third or so are playing 'seconds'. Gulp! Not content with playing the tune straight, some of these boys are playing harmonies! Here are real earth-people from places out east – *Uisgebhagh*, Port Pheadair … the great uncut – coming on to us newcomers with shakes, grips, strikes, taorludhs, 'bubbly notes' and birls. I am impressed.

I grit my teeth and pat my heart underneath my Harris Tweed jacket. I have to remember that, although I don't have the digital dexterity of these Uist children, I am going to play my two-bar fragment of the only 2/4 March I'm familiar with, not to challenge anyone but to uphold the honour of *clann Sheumais Mhòir*, the offspring of Big James Macdonald, in darkest Lochaber.

At the conclusion of the Jig, Duncan MacLellan dismisses the seniors. "*Sin sibh, a chlann*, There you go, children," he murmurs in valediction as he peers over his horn-rimmed spectacles and makes sideways flipping motions with his hands. "*Cuimhnichibh gun tèid agaibh air a' chiad phàirt dhen phort Donella Beaton a chluich nuair a choinnicheas sinn seachdain an-diugh. 'S e fear dhe na daoin' againn fhìn a rinn e – Seòras, mac Lachlainn Sionsain às An Iochdar*, Remember to be able to play the first part of the tune Donella

Beaton for next week. It was one of our own who composed it – George Johnson, son of Lachlan Johnson from Iochdar."

Weekly chanter practice is going to be hard.

Dòmhnall Iain Eàirdsidh, Donald John Macdonald from Torlum, had told me that I'd have to practise for three hours every night, but I didn't believe him – plus I believed I could handle that. Wasn't I from the epicentre of the universe? I'd definitely be able to take anything a humble crofter from the back of beyond could dish out, right?

"*Ceart, a chlann*, Right, children," *Donnchadh Ruairidh Dhonnchaidh* announces cheerily as he waves the younger kids forward to occupy the recently vacated chairs. "*Iarraidh mi oirbh, fear no tè mu seach, am port mu dheireadh a tha thu air ionnsachadh a chluich a-muigh an sheo air beulaibh chàich*, I'll ask you, one at a time, to come out here and play the last tune you learned in front of everyone."

I conclude swiftly that I'm not going to have any problems with this request. The truth is I know only two bars of one tune. I shan't have to agonise about what I'm going to play. Brown Hair Maiden wins it at a canter. I flirt briefly with the notion that I may top and tail my efforts on the practice chanter with a vocal rendition of the song itself. I'm beginning to feel slightly better already.

Inexplicably, everybody begins to cheer. Even people who are reluctant to cheer, like me who feels only a wee bit better, cheer once we see people cheering full out all around us.

"*Ailean Anna Ceit Uilleim*, Allan MacRury, Creagorry, playing Hugh Alexander Lowe of Tiree," a lad of about eleven or twelve calls out as he swaggers out to where our tutor is standing. Allan finishes this technically difficult four-part competition March with a stylish rallentando in the final couple of bars. The other kids whoop in appreciation.

A procession of technically accomplished boys and two girls follows this spectacular opener. They're all geniuses. Me? Well, up till this point I'd thought I was a pretty big deal because I could, with frequent pauses for breath, wiggle my fingers through two – two! – bars of a simple tune. These youngsters — MacPhersons, MacPhees, Macdonalds and MacMillans — rattle off Hornpipes, Reels and Strathspeys with aplomb. Mr MacLellan receives the musical pyrotechnics on display as no more than his due. He confines himself to mild congratulatory expressions like *'sgoinneil*, splendid' or *'cumhachdach*, powerful' at the conclusion of each recital. The *marag dhubh*, black pudding, I consumed at lunch time mulls in my stomach and my whole body tightens. Why are these kids doing better than me? Because they are better, that's why. These children from places like *Uisgebhagh*, Haicleit, *Port Pheadair*, generally referred to disparagingly by sophisticates from the west side of the island as 'muigh sa bheinn, out on the moor' aren't reading about Billy Bunter and the antics of the members of the Remove, whatever that is, at Greyfriars Public School. They don't dream of running away and joining the French Foreign Legion. These boys and girls out in the back of beyond have worked hard at their technique. They have been able to combine the hard work associated with life on the croft with an ability to compete at the same time. The inescapable conclusion is that I am not gifted. My father is wrong. I am average smart. But it's a mystery how I can be so ambitious and so lazy at the same time. I had fooled myself into thinking that being comfortable with words in two languages would equip me for the world. Other people were complicit in this ruse. Nobody told me I was just common or garden lazy.

Finally, it's my turn. I slouch up to the front of the group and propose to play my fragment of Brown Haired Maiden.

"De chanas iad riut, ille, What do they call you, boy?" Duncan

folds his lanky frame forward at the waist and makes his voice soft and concerned.

"'*S e Tormod MacGill-eoin an t-ainm a th' orm agus tha mi fhin 's mo mhathair a' fantail greis ann an taigh Sheumais Mhurchaidh an Griminis*, Norman Maclean's my name and my mother and I are staying for a while in James Macdonald's house in Griminish."

This is not the reply Duncan MacLellan wants to hear. It is my patronymic he seeks. Who is my father? Who was my grandfather? Already he must be aware that I am on a fleeting visit to the island and have no deep roots in the community.

"*Cà' do dh' ionnsaich thu a' Ghàidhlig*, Where did you learn your Gaelic?"

"*San t-Srathan. agus astaigh agam fhìn ann an Glaschu.* In Srathan and in my own house in Glasgow."

"*Càite an do rug thu air an fheadan an toiseach*, Where did you first take hold of a practice chanter?"

"*San t-Srathan*, In Srathan."

Cò chuir do chorragan air an fheadan an toiseach, Who placed your fingers on the chanter first?"

"*Mi fhìn …san t-Srathan*, Me …in Srathan."

"Uh-huh."

"*Mun tòisich mi air cluich, a dhuin uasail, am faod mi an t-òran a ghabhail an toiseach*, Before I play, sir, can I sing the song first?"

"*GABH AN T-ORAN, SING THE SONG …GABH AN T-ORAN, SING THE SONG … GABH AN T-ORAN*, SING THE SONG," the other kids yell.

Smiling broadly I launch into a very long version of the Gaelic love song.

Ho-ro, mo nighean donn bhòidheach, Ho-ro my brown-haired maiden,

Hi-ri, mo nighean donn bhòidheach, Hi-ri, my brown haired maiden,

Mo chaileag laghach, bhòidheach, My winsome, pretty maiden,

Cha phòs mi ach thu, You are the only one I'll marry.

The effect on the other children is instantaneous and very pleasing to me. I receive a standing ovation, boys and girls standing and clapping, beating tattoos on the teachers' table with palms and stamping on the linoleum floor with tackety boots and buckled patent pumps. Even Donnchadh claps his hands in appreciation.

"Siuthad ma tha, ill' oig, cluich am port a-nis, On you go, young man, play the tune now," our tutor commands.

(A technical description of my laboured efforts to reproduce the melody on the practice chanter employing false fingering will be boring to non-pipers and have only the fascination of a horror film to the thousands of orthodox pipers who abound in every continent of the globe. Suffice it to say that my unique version was pitched in C natural and involved the playing of the B note on the nine-note bagpipe scale by raising only the anular finger of my right hand.)

I whip the mouthpiece of the chanter from between my lips with a flourish and as I hear the first faint boos and jeers come from the audience a whirlwind of shame and action-spurring psychosis cycles through me. I know I shouldn't do what I do next, but I do it.

I sing the entire song for a second time.

Donnchadh Ruairidh Dhonnchaidh flares his nostrils. A girl covers her face with both hands. A tall boy in the middle of the semi-circle surrounding me laughs. Mr MacLellan looks at me open-mouthed and says softly, *"Chan eil fhios a'm carson a ghabhadh caileag laghach bhoidheach thusa, a laochain. B' fhearr leatha bhith ga sgròbadh seach gad èisteachd,* I don't know why a pretty, kindly girl would accept you, laddie. She'd prefer being flayed than listening to you."

So, to guffaws of laughter I turn to face my peers. Angus Macdonald from Torlum who later served in the Scots Guards raises his arms across the room like What? *Donnchadh Ruairidh Dhonnchaidh*, essentially a kindly man who is perhaps regretting his earlier sarcastic words looks at the back wall of the staffroom in order to avoid looking at me.

The world, which freezes for a moment, snaps back into action. I wave my practice chanter and run.

BACK TO THE BACKCOURT

When my father returned me to our 'hoose' at 191 Brand Street, back in June 1947, everything looked the same, only – at the risk of sounding self-contradictory – a wee bit different. The inanimate objects in the flat were familiar: the window overlooking the backcourt was still above the sink, cooker in the corner to the left, table bang in the middle of the room, father's 'big' chair next to the fire, cot jammed against the recessed bed, tallboy between the double bed and the door – all that stuff was as I had left it six years previously. It was the human inhabitants who had become more numerous.

Peigi Bheag, small and dark was either standing at the cooker to the left of the window or she was crouched over her Singer sewing machine at the far end of the kitchen table. She looked no different from the last time she'd visited me in Grìminis a year previously. She was the command centre of our household. Like *Eubhal or Beinn Mhor* and Teacla she was just there, unchanging and eternal. Then there was *Niall Mor,* my father, ashore for good now. He worked long hours and when he'd return late from his job as shore bosun with the Donaldson Line at Prince's Dock, he'd eat alone from a tray while seated in his 'big' chair by the fireside. He smoked like a fiend. When he coughed he worked up loose lung sediment. He didn't speak much, but when he did, everybody paid attention. He derived his pleasures from reading the evening paper, the Citizen, from front page to back, and listening to old 78s of Archie Grant.

Lorna, my young sister, born in a Catholic convent in Carmichael Street, Govan, three years previously, ran recklessly throughout the house. She was a chubby little curly-haired blonde who always had something to say and I hated her for it. Her accent was, as Glaswegians say, pure dead gallus Weegie, which didn't really astonish me since *Peigi Bheag* herself could transform herself from being a native of Cladach Baleshare, North Uist, to becoming archetypal working-class resident of Govan in a nanosecond. Without having been told about it, I understood that my mother had made a decision with regard to my sister. In direct communication with her infant daughter my mother had made up her mind to use English. She had accepted that Lorna would be like other second-generation city Gaels. Her daughter would understand Gaelic, because she'd hear it in the home, but if the wee one opted to respond in English, she, as her mother, wouldn't give a jot or tittle. Lorna was heading for a future where practically everybody spoke English. For that matter, so was I. Accordingly, I understood that it was demanded of me that I know colloquial Govanese as well as any idler who hung out at the Cross. I quickly acquired the spoken cadences of the majority of folk in Glasgow. Long story short: I learned to employ at least four distinct dialects in short order. I could switch from demotic Glaswegian to standard 'educated' English (at least the dialect favoured by, say, teachers) to nineteenth century spoken Gaelic to slick, 'modern' Gaelic, as spoken in Benbecula in the mid-twentieth century, within the click of a tongue. Conversations in our house were mind-shatteringly impenetrable, unless you were aware of the constant back and forth between dialects employed between residents.

"*A Nèill, thalla a-mach dhan 'Choperate' feuch am faigh thu buntàta is lof dhomh*, Neil, nip out to the Co-operative for some potatoes and a loaf for me," my mother would say.

"Don't think so, Peggy," my father would reply. "Got a meeting in the Pearce Institute tonight. *Leig le Tormod a dhol ann*, Let Norman go."

"*Cha tèid mo chas*, No way," I'd recklessly blurt out. "Homework tae dae."

"If you're going, Norman," wee Lorna would pipe up,"see and get me Jelly Babies."

"*Thu fhèin 's do* 'Jelly Babies, *a bhana-chèaird,*You and your Jelly Babies, you tinker," my mother would reprimand Lorna. "We hivnae coupons furr sweeties. *Dùin do bheil*, Shut up. *Ith na curranan th' air do thruinnsear*, Eat those carrots you've got on your plate.'"

"Aaww."

"It's a' right, Lorna," I'd say. "Ah'll bring ye back something nice fae the shoaps. Then I'd stretch out my hand to my mother. "*Thoir dhomh an t-airgead, a mhamaidh*, Give me the money, mammy."

"*Bu tu fhèin an gille*, Attaboy," my father would say.

My mother would hand me coins and a handwritten note.

"*Bheil gu leòr an sheo leis an ceannaich mi 'comic'*, Is there enough here for a comic?" I'd ask my mother.

"*Tha*, Yes," Peigi would reply with a sigh.

"No' be long, Lorna," I'd shout at my sister as I left the house.

This kind of four-way conversation was an everyday event in our household. Sometimes the conversations were five-way. The third adult to live in our 'hoose' – a one room-and-kitchen, mind – was my mother's youngest brother, Wee Colin. Built like a fly-weight boxer, stocky with foreshortened limbs, he had a comb-over and a very broad head with red folds bulging from the back of his neck. He stuttered badly and when he spoke, always in broad Glaswegian, and he made up for lack of fluency with increased volume. Inevitably, his contribution to the who-will-run-the-message debate would be something like, "It's a' right, Norman. Gie us the money an' Ah'll go" delivered in a stentorian bellow. I liked Colin – *creutair beag gun lochd*, a wee soul without sin, as my granny described him – and was more than happy to share the bed 'ben the room' with him. How I loved it when we performed callisthenics together on the carpeted floor! Before he left for work as a general labourer in Connell's Yard further along Brand Street, he'd encourage me to engage in the sit-ups, press-ups and stretching exercises he had learned during his army service in The Cameronians. The wee man was deeply concerned about encroaching baldness and he was a sucker for the 'treatments' offered in the Weekly News. The mantelpiece above the fireplace in our room was crammed with multi-coloured unguents and lotions. When left uncapped overnight after a diligent application these vials gave off pleasant whiffs of vanilla, apples and strawberries.

Life in this tenement tower of Babel was pleasant enough, but what really brought the roses to my cheeks was meeting other people outside the home. The boys in the 'back' soon accepted me into their wee gang, a membership that would have rather painful consequences.

It was in Primary 5, I really flourished. Because Bellahouston Primary School, next door to the Academy on Paisley Road West, was over-subscribed, the pupils in a couple of classes were decanted into Ibrox Special School, situated just off Edminston Drive, opposite Ibrox Stadium. Every Friday afternoon, Miss Craig would invite me to go out in front of my classmates and regale them with re-cycled tales of carnage and ghosts I'd heard in Lochaber and Uist. This was a new audience for me, a wee guy whose head was full of tales.

My entranced classmates were entertained with stories I had heard from my granduncle and older people in Benbecula: The Black Dog of Loch Arkaig and Gormshùil, the Witch of Lochaber, both got an airing, and were greatly appreciated by my urban audience. The Shieling of the Single Night, a horror story of bloody slaughter on Benbecula , had my listeners screaming, the boys naturally loudest. On her return from the office Miss Craig stood quietly behind me as I acted out the violent climax of The Tale of the Soldier's Coat. The resolution of this supernatural tale required me to provide sound effects. As I declaimed the words "… and young Angus retrieved the iron poker from the stove behind him, and brought it down with all the strength he could summon on to the collar of the blue coat which was jiggling unsupported before him. There came a loud BANG! …" I slammed shut the open lid of a vacant desk at the front of the classroom. A massed sharp intake of breath followed, greatly contributed to by the lady behind me. My peroration, delivered softly as a reasonable invitation, made clear that "I'll be delighted to act as guide to any volunteers who feel they'd like to rescue the abandoned Primus Stove and other camping equipment. Yes," I whispered, with all the insincerity of my tieless hero, "I'm willing to take all of you, if you like, to the site of the deserted shepherd's cottage in Knoydart, but …" I paused for a melodramatic beat. "I'll never set foot in the dwelling that contains the blue coat with the bullet-hole in the breast as long as I live." I restored the volume of my voice to cheery normal as I added: "And I want to live for a long time yet." The whoosh of released tension in the room was audible, some of it coming from behind me.

There followed a short period of shocked silence. The few girls I made eye contact with had that worshipping 'Oh, isn't he adorable!' look on their faces, and I immediately formed the thought that it wouldn't be a bad idea if I were to make a career out of this public speaking racket. The place suddenly went insane. Thirty-four boys and girls leapt to their feet and whooped and cheered me. Even the class bully, 'Cairnsie', and the geek who ultimately pipped me for the Dux Medal seven years down the line in the Secondary Department, Fred Ritchie, were jumping up and down and clapping enthusiastically. Miss Craig eventually restored order with some difficulty.

"Thank you, Norman," Miss Craig began. "You have a wonderful way with words. Your acting ability is impressive too." I wanted to ask her when she'd be called away from the classroom again, but she was already shaking my hand and inviting me to go back to my desk in the back row.

"Thank you, Miss Craig," I mumbled somewhat sheepishly and made my way through a thicket of outthrust hands from boys and girls who wanted to shake my hand or slap my back in comradely support. I made slow progress towards the double desk I shared with Ritchie, but a profound change had occurred in my life.

I was born to play with words, I thought. During this period, aged ten, I wrote my first novel, laboriously in longhand, and called it 'Torrie and the Comancheros Join the Legion.' I freely admit I had been obsessed by La Légion Etrangère since my return to Glasgow. On my imagination's screen I could easily bring up images of fortresses looming on desert sands, warriors approaching on horseback. I fantasized about meeting Beau Geste and joining a gallant group of fighting men who had erased their past identities and who, with self-formed personae, faced death with dignity. *Mmmmmm, a Thormoid.*

I remember reading all the Just William books by the age of nine. 'Torrie and the Comancheros' – surprise, surprise! – described the adventures of a gang of young Govan lads who marauded over the bosky parts of Glasgow's South Side – not the Gorbals or Hutchesontown, more Dumbreck and Pollok Park. The leader was called 'Torrie' – a variant of my forename in Gaelic – and the clan included an annoying young girl called Betty Elliot whose preferred method of messing with her stalwart leader's head was to threaten to have hysterics. I admit to owing a debt of gratitude to Richmal Crompton. The graver error I committed in my first venture into literary publication was the elementary mistake made by all aspiring authors. I imagined that what interested me would interest all readers. Despite the investiture of a huge amount of time and at least six bottles of Quink ink in actually writing in longhand my book in no fewer than six F2 jotters, financial returns were poor. The deal was that you could borrow the six notebooks for a week if you gave me two old pennies. I think by the time I left Craigton Primary School two years later – yes, our two classes were decanted yet again – to enter Preparatory One of Bellahouston Academy proper, I'd made about five shillings, 25p in today's currency.

Importantly for me I learned what I consider to be a valuable lesson. Words and arcane knowledge have their uses. They can gain you the affection of others. They can also alienate you from the affection of others.

AS OTHERS MAY SEE ME

A year after returning to Glasgow, I take up cigarette smoking in deference to my newly acquired membership of our wee nameless backcourt gang. My pal, Francis Aloysius Carrabine, who lives in the next close to us, at number 193, has secured an almost limitless supply of Passing Cloud fags after a sophisticated blackmail campaign directed at a young teacher in St Saviour's Catholic School (a sad man whose career with the Christian Brothers is a brief one.)

Anything worth doing, Franny and I must have agreed, is worth doing wrong. Maybe that is the basis of our philosophy on the afternoon my father catches us smoking in the rafters of our close entrance. Curiously, it is one poorly calculated act – the decision to indulge our burgeoning addictions so close to home – that initiates the nurturing of an erroneous belief in my own invincibility.

What we called 'the rafters' is a trellis of rough-hewn beams that criss-cross the entrance to our close: they are designed to protect our building from German bombs.

Consider our image. Imagine the coolness of it. Perched on our haunches on the topmost joists on either side of the close, we, the most charismatic lads within a quarter mile radius, puff and pass the oval-shaped cigarette from one to the other with accompanying gasps and sighs of satisfaction. A Protestant child and his Catholic counterpart, both still in Primary school, are bonding in a way that predates Pope John II's encyclical, Ut Unum Sint by forty-seven years. We are clearly boys who are ahead of our time. How prescient! How sweet! How dangerous!

It is unfortunate that in the very instant I am passing the half-smoked cigarette to Franny, my father enters the close. He's received another 'duck-egg': that is, he hasn't been chosen by the ganger at the daily 'line-up,' and rather than join his unlucky mates in the billiard halls of Lorne School and Kinning Park, he's decided to come home early. The sound of his footsteps on the three entrance steps to the close startles Franny and he fumbles the exchange.

The still-lit cigarette lands directly on top of Big Neil's bonnet and skitters in a cascade of sparks to land at his feet. He looks up, sees me and grabs me roughly by the calf and hauls me down to ground level. I am babbling senselessly as he wrestles me up the first flight of stairs ... Let me explain ... it was the boy I thought was my good friend who put me up to it. Yeah, he's a Catholic, you see, and he smokes a clay pipe his granny in Bunchrana gave him for his Christmas ... Know what? He's getting a box of cigars next year, so he is ... I only took a wee puff he brought to our close, and I didn't ... you know, swallow the smoke, did I?

My father stops on the first floor landing, still keeping a tight grip on the back of my collar. "*Greas ort*, Hurry up," he commands. "I'll deal with that wee Pape's family later."

Deal with the Carrabine family? Either the man doesn't know that Mr Carrabine was once a professional boxer and that Francis Aloysius Carrabine is one tough wee guy. He goes to the boxing at St Anthony's Chapel in Govan. Please, Franny, come down from the rafters. Get away from this close!

My silent prayer is half answered. Franny 'dreeps' from the rafters, but doesn't make for the close entrance immediately. He stands, feet apart, looking up at my father and me.

"Tell your dwarf of a father I'm coming round to have a word with him tonight," my father bellows. Big Neil has form when it comes to 'having a word' with the fathers of boys who have caused me harm. Alister Downie's old man has reason to remember Mr Maclean's visit to his home in Elizabeth Street. Alister, who was in the first year of Lambhill Street Secondary at the time, encouraged me to jump from the roof of a Wash House onto the sloping roof of a midden fully twelve feet away. The older boy assured me I'd do it in a 'waney,' or in one bound, but halfway through the leap I realised, too late, I'd need to do it in a 'twoey.' I crash landed on a pile of broken bottles and sustained a deep cut on my left knee that required ten stitches from Dr Mitchell. After a long period of rehabilitation – stitches broke frequently during periods of boyish exertion – I witnessed my father's invitation to Mr Downie to join him for a pint down in Howden's Pub. I also witnessed, a fortnight after that, our neighbour hirpling homeward along Ibrox Street on crutches.

Franny feels obliged to say something in response to my father's barely veiled threat. It amounts to a defiant squeal:

"Ach, yous are nothin' but a pair (perr) o' Proddie Dogs!"

I don't hear the rest of the exchange. My father grips my ear firmly between forefinger and thumb, and pain takes over.

The weird thing about Big Neil's flogging is the completely dispassionate way he disciplines me. He fetches the familiar razor-strop and orders me to take all my clothes off. (I've been busted before over milk money and foreign stamps and I quickly strip.) He then invites me over to the kitchen table – without a stitch of clothing on my trembling frame – and very calmly instructs me to eat some food he's laid out for me. I choke down as much as I can, and Big Neil informs me in cold, impersonal language that I have brought disgrace upon the family and will have to suffer the consequences. I am then placed firmly, but with a curious kind of tenderness, over the seat of an old wooden kitchen chair. He tells me to grasp the front leg of the chair with one hand and a rear leg with the other. A tin bowl is placed on the linoleum below my drooping head: to catch the vomit. Big Neil then, without haste, lashes his son's bare buttocks again and again with the razor-strop. Howling and gagging, I endure this humiliating torture in full view of my weeping mother and terrified, four-year-old sister.

After a time, he dresses the bloody wounds on my back and buttocks with gauze bandages dripping with a thick, yellow, viscous solution. Next he carries me through to the recessed bed in the back bedroom and leaves me there in the twilight for an hour or two.

There's something seriously wrong with this man. He batters me till I bleed. And then he comes over all tender. He'll be down shortly and he'll teach me phrases in Spanish, a language he acquired during his stay on the Argentinian pampas, where my Tiree grandfather broke horses for a living.

And I am right.

On the day after the flogging when I am still bed-bound, he buys for me a second-hand 'fairy cycle' in a matt black finish. To achieve this degree of intimacy my father first of all has to break the skin of my back and buttocks with a quarter inch thick razor-strop. Big Neil achieved intimacy by ricocheting between the savage and the tender.

I am stretched out on the double bed, face down, in a state between sleep and wakefulness. I sense my father standing gazing down at me. (My uncle, Wee Colin, who normally shares the bed with me has had to make do with a makeshift arrangement of sofa cushions and single woollen blankets for the previous three nights.) I pretend to be asleep.

An audience with my father without my mother being present is a rare event. He touches me lightly on the back of my neck. Or does he? Am I really about to have a conversation with my daddy or is this the kind of exchange I'd like to have and somehow I've willed this scene into existence?

"*Dùisg, a Thormoid*, Wake up, Norman," he whispers. "*Tha mi airson bruidhinn leat*, I want to talk to you."

Gingerly, I roll back until I am lying on my left hand side to face him. I am careful not to cause any friction between my bandaged waist and the bedclothes. If I move abruptly, the pain will be excruciating. Somehow I sense that my father's explosion of anger at what he considers a major transgression has burned itself out, and that I may have an opportunity to tell my side of the story.

There is a grim set to my father's mouth as he looms over me.

"*De tha ceàrr ort, a Thormoid,*What's the problem with you, Norman?"

"*Saoilidh mi nach eil dad ceàrr orm*, I don't think there's any problem," I say, genuinely puzzled.

"There's something I want to discuss with you."

"Uh-huh?"

"*Cuine chaidh thu nad chulaidh-bhùird as an sgoil agus air an t-sràid*, How long have you been a laughing stock at school and on the street?"

"I haven't been a laughing stock," I protest in English.

"You've been telling stories in front of the rest of the class, haven't you?"

"Well … I have been entertaining my classmates – and my teacher, Miss Craig – by telling them all the tales I heard in Lochaber and Uist."

Big Neil stares at me, his lips pursed. What is this man so serious about? What's wrong with telling ghost stories to the boys and girls in my class? They enjoy them don't they?

"*Dè mu dhèidhinn do chuid leughaidh, 's do chuid sgrìobhaidh, 's do chuid cùnntais?* What about your reading, your writing and your arithmetic?"

"*Tha mi a' toirt an aire dhan a h-uile sion as an sgoil,* I do pay attention to everything in school. I get top marks all the time."

"*Dè th' agad ri ràdh mun ghlaoicearachd that thu ris air an t-sràid,* What about all that clowning about on the street?" my father asks.

"*Dè rud,* What's that?"

"You've been seen marching round the block with that crowd of idiots you hang about with …chanting rude songs about Hitler and Himmler …pure rubbish, sgudal."

"*Bidh a h-uile duine gan seinn,* Everybody sings those songs."

My father makes an attempt at a smile, which is a slight but noticeable negative. His lips barely curl, the lower lip is thrust out in front to form a bus or pout.

"You're not everybody, Norman. *Cuimhnich air na daoine bhon tàini' tu,* Remember the people you're descended from."

"*A bheil coire sam bith ann a bhith togail do ghuth,* Where's the harm in wanting to be heard?"

"*Chan e coire a th' ann gu buileach,* It's not so much harm," Big Neil says reflectively as he scratches his cheek with his forefinger. "It's more how people will see you."

"*Tha an t-eagal orm nach fhaic daoine mi 's nach bi cuimhne aca orm an dèidh sin,* I'm frightened that people won't see me and won't remember me afterwards."

My father leans forward. He has thick, black eyebrows and grey stubble on his cheeks and chin.

"You think that smoking at your age will get you noticed?"

"Sometimes."

Big Neil sighs. "Why do have to be noticed?"

"You're not really living until people notice you," I blurt out as though I have rehearsed the thought for a long time.

"Well." My father turns his body away from the bed and

shuffles his feet to point at the door. *"Tha comas labhairt agad dha rìribh, ach chan e daoin' eile a leigheas an lot agad,* You've certainly got a way with words, but other people won't heal your wound."

"How do you know?"

"I was the exact same as you when I was young."

"How did you fix things?"

"Same way as you will. On my own."

He bends over the bed and shakes my hand with a hard, meaty grip. He turns to leave.

What? What kind of answer is that?

I begin to wail. "I just want to be seen and heard *los gum bi fios aig daoin' eile gu bheil mi beò anns an t-saoghal seo,* so that people will know I'm alive in this world."

A silent scream pierces my skull. Everyone out there, look at me. Listen to me, please. I exist in this world. I hear a faint click as the bedroom door closes behind my father and once again I am alone. I have been all along.

THE SLUMMIES ARE COMING

It is a fresh spring afternoon and I happen to be in the 'back' in the company of about ten local kids when we hear the preliminary battle cries of the invaders. Our kids are screaming 'The Slummies are coming! The Slummies are coming!'

"Don't just stand there like a spare, Norrie."

'Pudgie' Sutherland is twelve and he is warning a wee guy a year younger than him: me.

"What are you on about?" I say while keeping a 'tanner ba' up in the air using foot, thigh and forehead.

"The 'Slummies' are coming. Get up on to the dykes. They'll no' get ye up there."

Yet again, on the Ibrox-Govan border in Glasgow war has broken out. The backcourt of our red-sandstone tenement square is about to be invaded by an army of boys from the adjacent Slum Clearance housing scheme in Brand Street. The generals in this barbarian horde bear names like 'Gook', 'Pasha' and 'Fitzie' and are not to be messed with. These guys – well most of them – wear brass knuckledusters and carry bicycle chains and heavily-greased bayonets in steel scabbards. They have convinced our mob they'll be prepared to use them, and they enjoy terrorizing and inflicting pain on softer youngsters like ourselves whom they describe as 'toffs'. Already we can hear their scary ululations as they pour from the streets through the common closes which give on to the black, hard-packed earth of our territory. Their battle cry is a slow, five-note cascade of notes sounded to the vocable O – oh, oh, oh-oh, oh, corresponding to s, m, s-m, d. This is normally enough to send us all scurrying to the roofs of air-raid shelters, middens and communal wash houses. Once we are safely standing on our equivalent of the Golan Heights we fold our arms across our chests and try to look cool by squirting jets of saliva through the gap in our upper front teeth while waiting for the assembled ranks of armed savages to issue their invitation – always ignored – to come down to ground level and rumble.

I re-iterate: this was the normal procedure. For me, this is not a normal day. I don't scarper for the dykes like the rest of the lads. In this, as in so many other occasions in my long life, yes, I prove myself an idiot. Chin up, eyes narrowed in best Clint Eastwood fashion I stand my ground, a fearless chipmunk, in the face of the menacing advance of the dreaded leader, Mulrine.

Do you think, Norman your chipmunk impersonation honed in front of the lobby mirror will strike terror into Mulrine's heart?

This fourteen-year-old proto-psychopath stops about two feet away from me. He smacks a folded leather belt against the open palm of his left palm. This action causes his right bicep to escape from the rolled-up sleeve of the grubby collarless shirt he is wearing. There is revealed a mass of taut skin that hints at other patches of muscle beneath his soiled hand-me-down clothing. In a low-pitched gravelly voice he enquires: "You want some o' this?"

"No thanks. I'm not into masochism."

"No thanks!" Mulrine shrieks in high-pitched mockery. This passes for sophisticated banter among the Slummies. Sycophantic guffaws from his followers result. "You a poof?" he says.

I have an unclear idea of what the word means, but I just hate my tormentor's mean-spirited enunciation. And I've never been shy about employing half-understood language anyway. "Naw, I'm no' a poof." I say. Then, instead of putting a bridle on my tongue, I can't help blurting out: "May I reciprocate?" I ask. "Are you a poof?" Once again, my newly acquired mastery of the English language and my irresistible desire to show off my fast mouth had led me into jeopardy. This is not the last time that my tongue, as the Apostle James describes it in his salutation to the twelve tribes, will prove to be 'full of deadly poison'.

My pals on the roofs of wash houses, air-raid shelters and middens stare down at the madman below and wait to see just how bad things will get. They don't have to wait very long. He does not take kindly to a cheeky rejoinder from a runty little 'toff' and he bursts into violent action. He goes straight for my bare legs with the belt, slashing first viciously to his left and following rapidly with a whipped backhand to his right. I do the Watusi for a few seconds before holding my right palm in front of my face in an attempt to halt the beating.

"Hold on," I say in a muffled, whiny voice. I look my adversary straight in the eye and spread my hands to show that I am a reasonable fellow and unafraid. "I have a proposition for you. I'll tell you what I'll do with you ... if you'll just listen ..." I pause to get my breath back and to manufacture some conciliatory proposition which may appease the hissing wildcat in front of me. I have absolutely no idea what I am going to say next. And Mulrine isn't going to wait for me to say it. He grabs my ears, screaming, "You'll do nothing to me, ya bam!" and forcefully pulls my rather prominent nose towards his lowered close-cropped head.

This classic Glasgow kiss or head-butt causes copious gouts of blood to issue from my broken nose, and I hide my bitter tears behind splayed fingers while the crimson stuff drips onto the hard-packed earth. I sink to my knees. The velocity and ferocity of the many fists and boots, not just those of Mulrine, slamming down into my body make me curl up in the foetal position and sob uncontrollably.

What on earth made me expose myself to such horrendous pain? My initial, tentative diagnosis is that I overestimated the power of my rhetoric. I determine that this shameful episode will not haunt me for the rest of my life. I am acutely aware that if I don't learn how to defend myself, people – my own people – will say that I'm a 'cowardy, cowardy custard.' I don't want to give anyone the satisfaction of that. One witness to my predicament is my best friend, Francis Joseph Aloysius Carrabine.

"Franny, whit am Ah gonnae dae? Ah don't want tae hiv a' the other wans seein' me greetin'."

"Norrie, he said sympathetically. "Nothin' else furrit. Ye'll jist hiv tae come doon tae Saint Anthony's Boxing Club oan Wednesday night."

I look at him with keen interest. "Ye're right, Franny," I say. "Ah've goat tae dae somefin'."

I fear ending up crippled in the 'Deedle-Doddle', the Model Lodging House at the Govan Road end of MacLean Street in Plantation. With a broken nose, broken ribs and smashed knees I'll be unable to attend school. Uneducated, I'll be unemployed. Unemployed, I'll end up in the 'Model' doing what residents did in the well-known street song, sung to the tune of 'Springtime in the Rockies.'

When it's springtime in the 'Model',
The 'Model' in MacLean Street,
You can see the 'Lobby Dossers'
Washin' their dirty feet.

(Lobby Dosser: vagrant who beds down in a 'lobby' – the narrow gap between two 'single-ends.')

Govan Cross on a Wednesday night. At seven o'clock, forty-eight hours after the whipping from Mulrine: the grime-coated exterior of St Anthony's Roman Catholic church stands at the corner of Govan Road and 'The Golly.' Tentatively I climb the steps leading to a massive wooden door which stands slightly ajar at the entrance to the chapel. I'm slightly nervous as I push the great door fully open and enter a dark outer hallway with a gleaming white ceramic font in one corner. I hear a soft voice. It is an old priest, or so I guess, wearing a dark cassock and carrying a rosary in his right hand. Despite myself a Protestant street chant denigrating Catholics and their priests rises unbidden in my mind.

'O beads and beads and holy beads,
Beads and holy water (waaahter),
The priest fell doon the chapel stairs.
And broke his holy napper (naaaper).'

"Can I help you?" the old man asks.
"Yes, I want to learn how to … how to defend myself."
"Come with me, my son."

The man teeters forward in a stooped shuffle. I wonder how long these ancient looking priests have to struggle on offering Penance and Reconciliation or whatever it was that they do before they are allowed to hang up their cassocks. I eye the back of his head as I follow him into the church proper. For a short time I note his straggly grey hair and the loop of a silken green sash richly embroidered with gold thread which hangs round his neck. Then I look with amazement at my surroundings as we walk slowly up the central aisle. Blinding gold leaf is everywhere. The interior of St Anthony's church is so little like St Columba, Copland Road, where I attend Sunday School and the evening Gaelic service, it makes me feel inferior. In this place, St Anthony's Roman Catholic Church, Govan, The Word is to be delivered by a padre standing right in the centre of the stage. Stage left, there is a crescent of colourful plaster statues, the Virgin Mary, and a sample of saints I am unable to identify, and what I take to be a kind of choir box that goes from the back to the front of the stage. Behind the priest who may deliver The Word is a stained glass window depicting Jesus looking straight at the congregation with his sheltering arms outstretched, as if he were saying, "Come ye unto me."

"Follow me," the old man says looking back at me before veering right towards a set of double doors at the far end of the chancel. "I'm Father Ryan and I think we should have a little chat in the Recreation Hall." He inserts a large iron key into a bulky lock and one of the double doors swung open. We enter a medium-sized building whose brick walls are painted in leaf-green and tan. A few canvas and tubular steel chairs line three walls. The centre of the space is occupied by a real, kosher boxing ring. The old priest surprises me by sitting on the steps leading up to the ring. I remain standing in front of him.

Underneath bushy eyebrows barely two inches below his grey hairline his black eyes glisten. "What's your name, boy?"

"Norman Mac-"

"Norman?"

"Yes, sir. Norman Maclean."

"I've never seen you before. Are you a member of this parish?"

"Yes, I mean no, I live here in Govan, but I don't go to your church, I'm a …what I mean is … I'm a Protestant."

Father Ryan's eyelashes flutter rapidly. "Well," he says, drawing the vowel out, "I don't suppose there's any harm in a Protestant boy joining our boxing club, right? That'll be a decision for Gerry McMahon, our boxing coach, to make."

"I understand."

"Good," the old priest says, withdrawing a pocket watch

from somewhere below his ivory coloured surplice and briefly glancing at its face. "He'll be here shortly along with the rest of his charges."

"Great."

"He'll assess your suitability for training."

"When?"

"When what?"

"When will he assess me?"

"In about five minutes' time."

"What does he look like?"

"Why do you ask?"

"Well, I can wait for him outside."

"No, Gerry'll be here shortly. The old priest snapps open the lid of his watch once more. "Look, wait here. I have to excuse myself."

"Will that be okay?" I ask.

"Yes," he replies wearily. "I doubt very much you'll be interested in stealing one of our crucifixes, and I have my duties to attend to."

"Thank you."

I am tempted to make a run for it when he pauses in the doorway and turns towards me with a crooked smile on his lips.

"I don't suppose you'd like to take confession, would you?"

"Confession?"

"Yes, we offer the sacrament every evening for a two hour period."

"Naw," I pipe up hastily, and the word had scarcely left my lips, and instant regret follows. Maybe my curt refusal has queered my chances of getting into St Anthony's Boxing Club. Could I tell him I was Catholic? Could I fake it till I made it? How does the script go in the wee specially designed booth thing that I'd seen in films like The Song Of Bernadette?

'Forgive me father, for I have sinned ...'

Come on, *a Thormoid*, for a guy steeped in the *ròlaistean*, tall tales of *Seumas Mòr*, it shouldn't be too difficult to invent a few lurid sins, like – oh, I don't know – that I slaughtered a guy from North Uist with a scythe on Hosta machair some time ago but I now have only a vague recollection of the incident today. Will the lie about me being a Protestant constitute a sin? Ah, forget about it. My head's leaking with all these 'if only' and 'what if' subordinate clauses.

KALASHNIKOVS AND TRACTORS

As I await the arrival of Coach McMahon I have no idea that this man is going to encourage me to become a kind of machine. I am about to have a powerful metaphor imprinted on my consciousness. Can I, or any other youngster who wants to be a performer, produce the goods on demand, like a Massey Ferguson tractor, a Kalashnikov? When you turn on the ignition or press the trigger does the tractor or the rifle burst into life every single time? To be compelling as an exponent of a skill – fastest, strongest – you must embody the comparison-based achievement that we all revere in a completely unambiguous way

From where I am sitting on the ringside steps I see the double doors burst open and a dozen or so boys, ranging in ages from about eight to early teens, skip towards the ring and arrange themselves in an arc around me. I stare at them, moving my head slowly from left to right, and they stare back at me wide-eyed. Through the open double doors we all hear muffled voices coming from the chapel itself. Laughter … whooee … huggagh-huggagh … shinghin-shinghin … Maclean … tuh-unnnh! Tuh-unnnh!

Loud slapping sounds approached the entrance. Framed in the doorway stands a small figure wearing blindingly white sandshoes, tight black trousers and a nicely ironed open-neck white shirt. This has to be Coach McMahon. He is no taller than five foot six and cannot weigh more than 110 pounds, but thick in the chest. With shaved head and volcanic bearded face it is difficult to guess how old he is. He approaches us on the balls of his feet and glides through a couple of the boys until he stands directly in front of me, his face about a foot away from mine.

"Maclean?"

"Yes."

Without warning he fires a quick right hand at my face. I slip the punch with a jerk of my head and respond by raising my right fist as though to counter.

The trainer's leathery face breaks into a grin.

"Not bad, Proddie boy. Pretty good reflexes. We're going to improve on them, though."

And that was the start of it. I became a gym regular at St Anthony's Boxing Club. Within the sweat-stained walls of the recreation hall I spent a lot of time. The ring there gave me something that I didn't know I possessed. I discovered an ability to avoid being hit, and, perhaps more importantly, to endure long sessions of mind-numbing repetitive practice. For eighteen months Gerry McMahon would not allow me to don boxing gloves. He would loosely tie my hands together, either in front of me or behind my back, and loudly exhort the other lads, including my pal Franny Carrabine, to punch me as hard as they liked. "Hook him, hook him," he'd bellow. "Come on, Carrabine. Ye tellt me ye hid a dig. Show me whit ye kin dae tae this wee pansy." And the boys would take turns at flailing away at my head. I learned to move my head away when whoever was in front of me tried to poke me in the nose No matter how fast they tried to punch me I always moved my head out of the way in time.

Come on, Kevin ya bam, skelp that dirty Proddie's jaw for him. Holy Mother! Quick, Paddy, right cross, right cross. Naw, too slow. Whit's the matter wi' ye, Tony? Ye know he cannae hit ye back. Jab wi' the left, jab, jab, jab. Oh, forget it, Michael. He's too quick for ye, Brendan. Okay, keep slipping these punches, Maclean. And so on.

It was true that in the ring I seemed to know what opponents were going to throw, from where and at what angle, before they did themselves. After what seemed like an age, Coach McMahon decided to teach me how to counterpunch. It was slow cooking, but every Wednesday night for the next two years I threw punches. A right jab – for some reason I adopted a southpaw stance in the ring – would shoot out from a left shoulder twitch. The stiffer I could make it the better. A left hook, the kind that serves as an appropriate counter to failed right crosses, was perfected during extended bouts against different opponents. To do this effectively I performed a violently sudden hip twist. Uppercuts with either hand I learned in order to make myself a brilliant infighter. Overhand lefts, right crosses, nifty footwork, fighting off the ropes, all these moves I practised on the punch bag for hour upon hour until my muscles remembered on their own.

I also transferred this unthinking physical practice to my piping. For hours I would enter some kind of fugue state as I repeated on the practice chanter complicated digital movements like grips, doublings, strikes, taorluaths, throws on E, F and G', crunluaths, crunluathmachs, bubbly notes and back gracenotes on B,C and D. The improvement in my technique brought the roses to the cheeks of the Principal of the College of Piping, Seumus MacNeill, and grudging approval from my other tutor, Seonaidh Roidsein or Pipe Major John Macdonald of the City of Glasgow Police.

Yes, these repetitive exercises in my burgeoning career as a competing piper gave me some kind of profile among the ranks of the amateurs who used to blow their wee brains out at the Highlanders' Institute, Elmbank Street, the High School of Glasgow and the Headquarters of the Boys Brigade in Finnieston. Some of us — really gifted players like Iain MacFadyen, Norrie Gillies and Arthur Gillies from Taynuilt — ventured further afield to competitions in more exotic locales like the Cowal Gathering and Highland Games in places like Airth, Cupar, Caol and South and North Uist.

In short, the obsessive-compulsive drive for improvement in the contrasting pursuits of boxing and piping were validated only in the latter when I started to creep into the prize lists at junior competitions. Oddly enough, I never had an amateur boxing career. While Franny Carrabine and all the Pats, Micks and Kevins were encouraged to enter inter-parish boxing tournaments, and acquitted themselves very well at these events, Coach McMahon would not let me board the team bus. I braced him about my exclusion from competition one Wednesday night.

"I was wondering," I said, "when I'd get my chance."

"What chance?"

"You know, to fight for the club."

"You? Fight in the sacred vest of St Anthony's?"

"Yes," I replied defiantly. "Nobody can lay a glove on me, right?"

"Maybe."

"So, what's the problem?"

Gerry McMahon, he of the deep chest and square jaw, a legend who had lasted for ten rounds before being knocked out by the great Benny Lynch in a savage bout in the Grove stadium in Finnieston in the thirties, peered down at me with a puzzled expression on his face.

I attributed my ban not to ability or lack of it but to anti-Protestant bias on the part of the clergy serving in St Anthony's at the time. I really ought to have conned old Father Ryan into believing I was Catholic. I should have taken confession that first day. I should have asked the old boy if it was okay to take food and maybe a sleeping bag into the booth as I had so much bad stuff to tell him. I volunteered to go as a supporter of my teammates, but McMahon would not be swayed.

"Maclean?"

"Yes, Coach."

"What I'm telling you, son is that, wi' all possible apologies, I have to report to you as a member of St Anthony's Boxing club, you are suspended."

"Why? I don't think I understand what 'suspended' means."

"I'm afraid it means the ba's oan the slates fur somebody like you."

"Ye mean I'm bombed out here after all this time?"

"That is unfortunately right."

"What," I said, "you mean I'll never be able to box for the club?"

"Oh my no, if you keep your nose clean, keep practising, there may come a time when they'll lift your suspension."

"Who are they?"

"Well, it's really a he."

"Father Ryan?"

"Maybe."

"Can I speak to him?"

"No."

"Why not?"

"He can't speak to you."

"Is it because I didn't take confession that first night?"

"No. I mean he's not here. He's gone."

"Can I make an appointment to see him when he gets back."

"No, he's away for good."

"He's chucked his job? Any idea where he is now?"

"He led a pure, blameless life, so he did. I'm pretty sure he's in a good place now."

"You're saying … what?"

"He slept in the day."

"It's half past eight now. Can you not get him up?"

"No, I'm saying he slept in …for good."

"What are you telling me?"

"He's pan breid."

"What?"

"Deid. Nae mair confessions, communions and a' that fur Father Ryan."

"I'm sorry."

"It's no' your fault."

"Right …but what about my suspension?"

"It's whit we call 'sine die', son. Here in Govan when Father Ryan decides on something, like your case, it's like when His Excellency makes a pronouncement in the Vatican. It's the law, son."

Finally, I see myself getting steadily getting more fed up with McMahon's obfuscation, turning on my heel and breaking into a trot. I know I am leaving St Anthony's for ever. I stop at the double doors and make my valediction.

"If you ever change your minds about the 'sine die', tell Franny Carrabine about it and he can inform me. Right now I'm trapping."

"Wait, son!" The Coach is walking towards me waving the pair of boxing gloves I always wore in the ring.

"Naw, I really have better things to do, Coach."

"At least take the gloves."

"No, sorry. Sorry, no. I'm off."

"That wisnae mah decision, Maclean."

"This is mine, though. I'm away home. I'm a busy guy … lots to do."

"Whit better things hiv ye tae dae at hame?"

"Playing my bagpipes." For the life of me I cannot come up with any other activity at home that demands my attention. I turn and sprint towards the main building and the freedom of Govan Road.

Outside I slow to a jog, then to a slow walk. I make up my mind never to enter a boxing ring again. Of course, I don't stick to it. Fast forward a decade to 1959 when, fighting at Light Heavyweight in the colours of Glasgow University, I was pummeled into unconsciousness by a hirsute Irishman within the first two minutes of round one.

WAR AND PEACE

"Kiltie, Kiltie cauld bum, Big banana feet, Went to the pictures, And couldnae get a seat." Malky Cairns from the 'pen' close in the Holy Lawn croons softly behind me as I accept a beautifully weighted pass from Ian Dougall in the region of the centre spot. It was a couple of minutes from full time during an eleven-a-side trial football game on one of the three full-sized cinder pitches fronting McLellan Street (the longest continuous, unbroken street in Glasgow) and adjoining Plantation Park.

Three figures stood along the touchline. Slightly apart from two adults, 'Beef' Macdonald, another tenement teuchter like myself — although barely fourteen, but five-eleven and a lummox in appearance — walked stiffly up and down the touchline as though he had a keg of lager between his legs, his face tight with anger. The two gentlemen, one in baggy navy sports top and cotton pantaloons with silver stripes along the outer seams, the other in a three-piece grey herring-bone suit, stood on the sidelines. The one in sports gear was Mr Morris, Senior Physical Training Instructor at Bellahouston Academy, and the suit was Mr Stewart, an Assistant Teacher of Mathematics in the same institution. The former was present because he always involved himself in all the extra-curricular sporting activities held under the aegis of the school; swimming galas, athletic meetings, football, hockey and rugby games. The latter was observing proceedings keenly through gold rimmed spectacles because he had been nominated by the Depute Headmaster, Duncan ('Husky Bill') McLean, to be responsible for taking care of and, more importantly, choosing the players who would for the next three terms represent the school's Fourth Eleven. An additional qualification held by Stewart was that he was reputed to have played professionally for Third Lanark FC before the Second World War. He was the guy I had to impress in this week-long series of trials if I were to gain a place on the Fourth Eleven squad.

I was struggling because of the unwanted attentions of Malky Cairns from the 'pen' close on the Holy Lawn. This building at the corner of Midlock Street and Paisley Road West whose derivation probably had something to do with Irish immigrants who flocked to the city in the mid-nineteenth century was demolished in 1959 and the Ibrox District Library and an Islamic Madrasa now stand on the site. A 'pen' close was a large gap in a tenement building, a dark unlit alleyway, from which two entrances, one each on either side of the cobbled lane, led via spiral staircases to at least four landings. Each landing embraced three hallways which were always locked in Stygian gloom. Anyone entering one of these hallways, known as 'lobbies', would dimly perceive on his right and on his left a scarred wooden door with a nameplate, letter-box and numerous locks. Behind each door was a single room containing a fireplace, cooker and a double bed recess, perhaps with a rickety settee in the centre of the room. This ten feet by fourteen feet rectangular box accommodated families of upwards of six members. A communal toilet served all six households on each landing. These dwelling houses were known as 'single ends'. There was a stigma attached to the names 'pen close' and 'Holy Lawn'. If you were associated with both, it was like saying you came from Sodom and were familiar with Carstairs Prison for the Criminally Insane. The star alumnus of the Holy Lawn was a youth called Malky MacRae, whose grandparents had emigrated to the city from Skye at the turn of the century. Malky was a notorious troublemaker who wore velvet-collared, American-style zoot suits with one memorable fashion accessory: the handle of an open shaving razor ostentatiously protruding from the breast pocket of the jacket. Rumour had it that he had given a rival gangster from Kinning Park two facial 'Mars Bars' (scars) that required twenty-two stitches.

All twenty-two first year trialists were scurrying from end to end of the pitch, chasing the ball and paying scant attention to making measured passes to team-mates in better positions. It was all – bango! – a hefty boot upfield and – tally-ho! – a pack of yellow-bibbed youngsters scooting in pursuit and another scrum of opposing players wearing blue bibs converging on the ball. The only lad who seemed to be able to read the game and who generously made passes to his forwards was a red-head called Dougall Among the entire first year intake Ian Dougall was The Man. Everything coming from the yellow tops revolved round 'Ginger' Dougall.

He it was who had stroked the full-sized leather 'bladder' towards my feet a few seconds earlier. Unfortunately, Malky Cairns was all over me, almost lying on my back, clicking my heels and going, "Mrs MacLean had a wee wean, She didn't know how to nurse it. It wanted a feed, so she gave him some breid, And its wee belly burst-ed."

This pest just wouldn't stop! 'Cairnsie' was a tall, skinny boy with whippet bones, thin, dun-coloured hair cropped Roman-emperor style over low pimpled forehead; no lips, chips of dull slate for eyes, cheekbones like tomahawk blades. I immediately sketched a biography for this denizen of the 'pen close' at the Holy Lawn. He'd definitely be stabbed or 'plunged' in a back alley behind a wine-moppers' bar in Tradeston or Cowcaddens.

After the referee, a tall sixth former, blew the whistle to bring the nightmare of a game to a close, I plodded off the field, head down, totally whipped.

'Beef' strode towards me. "Hey, *a Thormoid*," 'he said. "That bampot Cairnsie wis gi'ein' ye a rough time, wisn't he?"

"Uh-humh," I grunted as I shrugged out of my yellow bib and added it to the pile already cradled between his brawny forearms. Without explanation and with no wish to expand on the subject I walked from the touchline of the football pitch towards the ramshackle dressing rooms to retrieve my school satchel and make my mournful way home for tea. I was dying to look at the two adult male teachers who were conferring earnestly around twenty feet away, but I didn't.

"*Trobhad seo, ille*, C'mere boy," Beef commanded.

"What?"

"Ah'm comin' up tae yours furr a wee ceilidh the night," the young giant announced.

'Beef' was the son of *Iain mac Anna an t-Sealgair*. That is, his father, originally from North Uist, was the grandson of a long deceased character called The Hunter. I attributed epic qualities to this mythical character. Without a soupcon of evidence I had The Hunter pegged as a bold traverser of *Eubhal* and *Beinn Mhòr* with his 'slim gun' and deer hounds at heel. His progenitor's genes were clearly present in 'Beef'. Everything about this young man was gigantic. His skull was the size of a leather 'bladder', no a medicine ball, with squinty little eyes and a narrow mouth and a couple of nostrils stuck roughly in the middle of his wide face, and no neck at all. From the ears down he was just one solid welded hulk, the size of a fridge-freezer. I had the idea that 'Beef' MacDonald came from a whole other species, he was so big.

Only boys with Highland or Island lineage were afforded the privilege of being invited into Peigi Bheag's 'room and kitchen' at

191 Brand Street. *Feadhainn Ghallda*, or Lowland Strangers, were never invited into our house. My pals who knocked on our door to invite me out to play were invariably left standing outside while I was summoned. The offspring of Màiri Fhraochain from Loch Carnan, in South Uist, Big Iain MacGibbon or his beautiful sister Isabel whom I secretly fancied, or of Jimmy and Kitty Martin from Islay, were ushered into our kitchen with gracious ceremony and invited to share in whatever meal we might be enjoying. It was as if our particular tribe was proclaiming our separate identity by observing a strict totemic system.

'Beef' was favoured. He settled into my father's easy chair, accepted the cup of tea and Blue Riband chocolate biscuit offered by my mother and began to speak.

"Now don't forget," he intoned in an unnatural double-bass. "When you turn up for the trials tomorrow, make sure you sling these daft sannies you wear. You'll be wearing my football boots. Ah'm gonnae lend you them – just for the day …tuigsinn?"

"But, 'Beef'," I protested weakly, "I only take a size five …I'd drown in your boots."

"Dùin do ghab, amadain, Shut it, you fool," was the response. "We"ll stuff them wi' newspaper so they'll fit, ma tha, and you'll have enough weight to make it count when ye kick 'Cairnsie'."

"Ah'm gonnae kick 'Cairnsie'?"

"Aye, efter you smash him in the belly wi' yer elbow … tuigsinn?"

I let his voice, one broiled in scalding hot mugs of Bovril and Woodbine cigarettes, roll over my head.

"I don't want you, *a Thormoid*, to be scared of that skinny prick," 'Beef' continued solicitously. "You'll smash him in his solar plexus with all the strength ye've got in that wee body o' yours … tuigsinn? And that's him on the deck, ma tha. Then, whit ye dae is kick him oan his ankle." His face which had been wearing an expression of disgruntled misgiving suddenly cracked into a derisive laugh. "He won't be playing much football after that ... *ceart*?

I drank in his performance like tiger's milk for, as it were, my schizophrenic soul. I loved the tone of his voice, which was 'Glesca' Gallus' sprinkled with rhetorical Gaelicisms. I loved the *tuigsinns, ma thas* and the odd *ceart*. They were so, somehow ... other ...so different ...so metrical.

"What ye've got to realise, *a Thormoid*," 'Beef' enunciated with extreme clarity in the painfully slow and fulsomely stressed tones of an infant teacher in a remedial class, "is that we're different from the Goill. We're better than them ...*tuigsinn*?" He placed a forefinger against his button nose. "Say your team hiv got a corner kick, *ceart*? 'Ginger' Dougall lobs the ball into the penalty spot. You're just one of aboot twelve boys who're tryin' to heidy the ba' ...*tuigsinn*? "Cairnsie's behind you, ceart? Baith o' ye jump up. Forget the ba'. Make sure the ref. cannae see ye. Ram yer elbow straight back and throw a' yer eight stone intae yer thrust ...*tuigsinn*? He'll go 'Ooooooooof' and drop like a stone. Ye've elbowed this annoyin' nuisance right in the solar plexus! Ye've ... decked ...the enemy, *ceart*`? Noo, as the coup de grâce – "

Coup de grâce? I couldn't believe it. 'Beef' Macdonald was sitting in my father's easy chair saying "coup de grâce"? I wondered if he had rehearsed his sermon.

" – whit ye dae is wheel round and belt him, full force, wi' the boot Ah'm gonnae gi'e ye as a gift. Skelp him wi' that good right foot o' yours, on his ankle ...*tuigsinn*?"

'Beef' stood up and walked towards the kitchen door. He turned and delivered a grave valediction. "Remember, *a Thormoid*," he said, "we're living in a town that's no' as real as, say, Uist or Lewis. Daliburgh is real. Shawbost is real. If these places are real, then Glesca's just a made-up story. Know'm saying?"

I carried out 'Beef's' instructions to the letter. I crippled 'Cairnsie', got into the fourth eleven and was elevated to the

Glasgow Schools' under-sixteen team three years later. I tell you: I didn't feel like a hero.

Now, my life wasn't all brutal violence during my first year of secondary education. What a busy little boy I was when I was chosen to join Class 1SL (Special Latin) in Bellahouston Academy! I was turning into quite a wee swot. (Did I mention that in Primary Seven I was offered bursaries to attend 'Hutchie' Grammar, Allan Glen's and the High School of Glasgow? Predictably, I knocked these potentially rewarding opportunities back, because, fond as I was of cutting a sartorial dash, I dreaded the prospect of turning up for our 'three and in' football games in a posh blazer and fancy school cap.) Anyway, 'Bella', as we called those Gothic walls and turrets on Paisley Road West didn't disappoint. I learned Latin and French and lapped up Mathematics and Science and shared first prize for English composition with Joan MacSwan, a grounded girl of Skye descent. I mauled Caesar's Gallic Wars and couldn't get enough of Palgrave's Golden Treasury. Latin proved to be a life-saver. Private schools have long known that Latin and Greek give their pupils an intellectual edge. I thought in the early stages of studying Latin , despite my very early exposure to Book IV of the Aeneid in the arms of my father and the presence in the class of Flora McIntosh, a stand-out beauty whom I fancied something rotten, the declension of nouns and the conjugation of verbs was completely useless. A couple of terms into the subject, however, I realised the extent to which Latin had not only expanded my cultural horizons but had also given me a secure grip on English and other languages.

Of course, the highlights of my week were the Monday and Thursday piping tutorials I received from Seumus MacNeill of the College of Piping and Pipe-Major Seonaidh Roidsein of the City of Glasgow Police. Extra-curricular activities included bird-watching on Neilston Pad with the Walker brothers from Elizabeth Street, regular Saturday morning football matches against first year teams from schools like Lenzie Academy, Queen's Park, Hyndland, St Gerard's Secondary, Govan High, and Holyrood Secondary. I have to admit that when I started to carry a copy of Waldren's Latin-English Dictionary onto the team bus, the other lads tended to avoid me.

GRUDGE BOUT

I kind of forget about my run-in with Mad Malky. Malky Cairns doesn't forget about me, though. Word trickles slowly but steadily through intermediaries that the Holy Lawn is in forment.

"Cairnsie's comin' tae get ye, Norrie," Jamesie Crawford, a classmate who lived in a dimly lit close at the intersection of Ibrox Street and Whitefield Road, confides to me one day at Registration. "Says he's gannae gi'e ye a doin."

I adopt the 'do nothing' method of response, taking care to assume the Govan dialect. "Him and whit army?" Somebody tells me about a threat and I do nothing.

Threats from the Holy Lawn intensify. There's a crowd of us huddled together in a back close in a tenement adjacent to where I live.

"Hey, Norrie," Jim Bannan says. "Want tae smoke some cinammon stick?"

Oh, this is what you do with these crumbly, brown cylinders you buy in Stark's sweetie shop in Ibrox Street. You don't eat them – they do taste a wee bit 'foosty' – you're meant to smoke them like cigarettes, are you? A quick recap of what I know about smoking at this time. My father smokes heavily: at least two packs of Lucky Strike when he was home on leave and now, having left the sea and with a job as a shore bosun , he makes do with twenty Capstan every eighteen hours.

"Did you know, Norrie, that Cairnsie's runnin' amok the noo?" This from a fair haired lad called Bobby Walker who comes from Kirkwood Street right across the Paisley Road from the Holy Lawn. I resent slightly that this outlander has somehow migrated up behind me.

"Yeah, he's declared war on the Skene Road gang," Bobby walker amplifies his information.

"So?"

"Says he's gonnae destroy you next."

I put on a stern John Wayne type accent – "That two-bit bandit thinks he can turn a blind eye to the law and ride into my town and terrorise the good people of Brand Street, but Sheriff Maclean will show him the light and dump him on his backside."

All the puffers of cinammon break up. "Ye're a good laugh, Norrie," Iain MacKenzie says.

"I know. I give everybody a great time. But I'll give Cairnsie a really bad time if he ever comes near me."

My big pal Iain MacGibbon, *an gille aig Màniri Fhraochain*, Mary daughter of Heather-top from Loch a' Charnain, approaches me a couple of days later.

"Norrie, did you know that Cairnsie goes tae a specialist clinic up the toon?"

"Whit furr?"

"Manic-depression."

"Manic-depression?" I feel a stab of something like envy. These guys get to enjoy the manic episodes. "Whit urr ye tellin' me this furr, Iain? D'ye think ah'm feart o' him?"

"Maybe ye should be, Norrie. This fella, if he's a maniac, could hurt ye ...bad."

"Oh, Iain, ye're so cute, man!" I coo at him so patronisingly.

"D'ye forget ah went tae the pineapple, the chapel yous yins go tae, St Anthony's in Govan, to learn how tae box?"

Not everyone is as confident of my chances. 'Pudgy' Sutherland from low-down in 189 Brand Street has some advice for me.

"Listen, Norrie," he says with a serious expression on his face, "Ah think you'd benefit from seein' somebody."

"Whit d'ye mean?"

"Like, you know, seeing somebody."

"Aw, aye – know whit ye mean. But ah'm no' a' that good at chattin' up girls."

"Girls! Naw, ah mean sookin' up tae Jackie Connor, the leader-aff o' yon Plantation Crew. Ye need allies, Norrie. Ye should start seein' a gang leader."

"That's san ferry-ann (*ça ne fait rien*) furr me, George. Ah'll haunle (handle) this masel', thanks."

A more useful suggestion comes from 'Scotia', Iain Scott, who was a sergeant in the 103rd Glasgow Company of the Boys' Brigade. He runs a kind of youth club in the recreation hall of Bellahouston Parish Church on Carillon Road every Saturday night. Activities range from snooker, table tennis to light sparring with old boxing gloves that have seen better days. I avoid the last pastime and spend my time listening to singles from American pop singers like Johnnie Ray, Frankie Lane and Doris Day and scampering round both the ping-pong tables and the full-sized billiards table.

"Got a minute, Norrie?"

"Yeah."

"Ye know ye'll hiv tae fight Cairnsie sometime, don't ye?"

"Aye. Suppose so."

"Ah've goat an idea."

"Whit?"

"How d'ye fancy hivin' a boxing match wi' him at the BB Club some Saturday might?"

"Cairnsie's no' in the BB.'

"Leave that tae me. Wid ye be willin' tae box fifteen rounds wi' him? We widnae hiv ropes or that, but we'd mark oot the ring wi' tape. Ye'd baith hiv new gloves and there'd be stools and buckets an' that in yer coarners. And ye kin pick yer ain seconds an' that. Whit dae ye say?"

"Awright."

"Ah'll speak tae Captain MacNichol aboot it …get his permission, like …and we'll settle furr the last Saturday of the month, okay?"

"Sure."

We shake hands. We look into each other's eyes as we shake. I see excitement in his. I wonder if he detects fear in mine.

I have my interview with Captain MacNichol the following Saturday evening in a brightly lit kitchen where Scotia will make Bovril and heat mince pies halfway through proceedings. We sit on kitchen chairs knee to knee.

"All right, now, here's a very important question – Captain Mac Nichol leans forward – do you really, really want to box fifteen rounds against this … this young Cairns fellow?"

I sense that this is a very important question. It might be the kind of question that determines whether I get to finish my stellar academic career at Bella or at a school for the disabled.

"Yes," I articulate with difficulty. "I don't hate him."

"He hates you."

"Cairnsie basically hates everybody.'

Captain MacNichol stands up. "Well, Maclean, good luck."

It's clear that this is going to be the biggest event in the history of the 103 BB. Boys are whispering about this grudge match in the playground of Bellahouston Academy and the surrounding streets.

Did you hear about the fight?

Aye, at the BB Club a week on Saturday.

Cairnsie's a psycho.

Aye, but Norrie's been tae the boxin' at St anthony's.

Somebody's gonnae end up in the Sufferin' General.

As Pudgie Sutherland, my chosen second, laces up my gloves, I sit back on my stool and try to avoid looking at the opposite corner where Malky Cairns of the Holy Lawn is sprawling, none too clean khaki shorts on his skinny legs, and scratching everything with his gloved hands – his face, chest, thighs – as he mumbles to his second and sways from side to side. His second – Aw naw! - is the dreaded Malky MacRae, sans jacket, and presumably cut-throat razor.

The packed spectators are yelling. What they are yelling for is blood – 'Blood Bath, Blood Bath" – and what they're getting from me is totally ignored.

"Norr-ie! Norr-ie!"

As we stand in the centre of the makeshift 'ring', Malky Cairns and I engage in staredowns – these ritualistic exercises peculiar to boxing where the two opponents will stare at each other with only a short space between them with neither fighter willing to blink first. Scotia is explaining the rules in a rapid monotone. The whole thing is extremely silly. This is, after all, a game where you can legally punch your opponent on the chin if he annoys you too much.

Boxers and enthusiastic audience get one of those charged moments before the starting bell rings and the worlds of the fighters begin to expand to embrace the infinite possibilities that may be actualized in the coming minutes. It's a funny old game, the boxing. There's no guarantee for either fighter. The match can be over at any second, and potential embarrassment lurks round every punch and counter-punch. Clearly, a voice sounds in my head. Cairnsie is a fool for seeking revenge. So am I for my agreeing to reciprocity.

After the bell rings to start the fight, Cairnsie and I meet in the middle of the ring and warily circle each other. We both miss. No punch lands. We are both reluctant to open up, wary of the other's counterpunching ability. The silent spectators see that, although he isn't close to landing it, Cairnsie's left jab is very quick. Halfway through the first round shoots out a right that I avoid easily. But, as I raise my head back into position, Cairnsie lands a short left hook to the head that knocks me temporarily off balance. This is a wee bit of a brasser. Even more of a brasser is the left jab to my ear at the end of the third round that almost drops me on my face. I shake my head and smile to show I am not hurt. I wake up in the fourth round, never getting hit significantly and landing good, hefty left hooks to the body.

The next few rounds are slow with neither of us establishing a clear lead. For me, it isn't going too badly, but it isn't going too well either. In the ninth round Cairnsie's mouth is open. He is tired. I am not. Have these Sunday route marches at our annual camp in Benderloch anything to do with my superior stamina? At the head of a column of cadets I've blown my bagpipe without stopping all the way from the Parish Church in that Argyllshire village to our camp site at MacDonald's Farm on the Bonawe road, well over a mile.

Thanks to Coach McMahon at St Anthony's I have learned to pace myself. I know I am slightly stronger than my opponent. In the tenth, Cairnsie's tired hands are down, that is in the intervals when he isn't throwing wild, amateurish punches that further betray his fatigue. It's a strange thing about boxing: rookies always think that the greater the distance a punch travels the more damaging it will be. Not true: knockouts are never delivered by bringing the glove up off the deck in a wide sweep upwards towards an opponent's jaw. Economy of movement is the secret.

Cairnsie's getting careless. In the eleventh round I catch him with a hard left hook that hurts him and sends him over the taped extremities of our 'ring' where he stand, gloves at his sides, breathing heavily. I abandon the 'leftie' stance and quickly revert to the orthodox approach. After a barrage of stiff left jabs I pause for a split second, feint with my left, and shift my weight perfectly. I then throw the best punch I will ever throw, an overhand right that lands flush on Cairnsie's exposed left jaw. He straightens from his crouch briefly, shudders and drops on his face.

Scotia is counting to ten. I raise my arms in the universal boxing sign for I won. A storm of raucous celebration from the massed ranks of my supporters in the 103rd Glasgow Company of the Boys Brigade breaks out.

"Ooooooh!"

"Good on ye!"

"Wheeeeeeeh!"

"Gaun yersel, Norrie!"

"Norr-ie! Norr-ie!"

"Ewwww!"

I am a sort of alpha male now, but I know, deep down, I'm a schneider. Poor Cairnsie is on his feet now being supported by his second. He totters forward towards me on hollow legs and extends his arms. He hugs me. It is a man hug, complete with slapping, and for a brief moment I am jubilant. The feeling doesn't last long. I am hoisted away from Malky's embrace by enthusiastic supporters. The whooping and shouting starts to spiral downwards as I am carried into the kitchen where Captain MacNichol is seated at the table. He dismisses the other boys and invites me to have a seat next to him. I indicate that I prefer to remain standing.

"You know, Maclean," he says excitedly, "that was as good a knockout punch as I've ever seen. How are you feeling?"

"Not too great, as a matter of fact."

"What's wrong?"

"Ach, I don't know. All I know is, that punch was a bit of a fluke. Ah'll never be able tae repeat it."

"But, Maclean."

"Ah don't want tae repeat it. Ah'm gonnae gi'e this boxing lark the elbow, know whit ah mean?"

I was aware that my victory would make me gold-plated in and around Bellahouston Academy. Members of other wee gangs like the 'Copie' from Copland Road and the 'Lambie' from Lambhill street would hear about the perfect punch and would attribute to me fighting prowess I didn't actually possess. If some of the lads I came into contact with believed I had fists of iron, I was willing to let them do so. All I wanted was a degree of freedom to allow me to pursue other interests. These goals were still vague and undefined, but I knew they were out there.

"Your choice, Maclean," Captain MacNichol says, making a sound through his nose as though he's about to sneeze. "What do you intend to do, if you give up the boxing?"

"It's not all that clear to me as yet," I say with all the sincerity I can muster as I look straight into his eyes. "I want to do something – oh, this is embarrassing – something with my brain."

The Captain of the 103rd Glasgow Company of the Boys Brigade stands up and extends his hand. I grip it in manly fashion and shake it vigorously to intimate that I am almost an adult and that from now on I'll plough my own furrow. Events did not exactly crystallise in the way I'd described to my old BB leader.

THE BOSOM OF THE GENTILITY

It wasn't as if I hadn't been told that smoking was a sucker move. Back at the beginning, younger members of our wee gang and I would cluster in groups of five or so in air-raid shelters and pass round a lit cinnamon stick. Older guys would join us now and again and fire up real cigarettes. I remember Iain Macdonald, who must have been three years older than the rest of us fixing me with a beady eye and saying,"You know, Norrie, the way ye're sookin' on that cinnamon stick, ye're gonnae hiv a Capstan cigarette in yer wee mooth afore ye're very much aulder." I dismissed the notion at the time, but Macdonald was correct. Shortly afterwards, one of the guys breezed into Marguerite's Sweetie Shop in Gower Street across the road from our school and asked for a 'single'. These came from a broken packet and cost two old pennies. Our daredevil cowboy handed over the two coins and explained that the cigarette was for his 'faither'. The profits derived from the lucrative school playtime trade account for Marguerite's willingness to serve under-age kids. No father ever received a single cigarette. A 'single' was for wee boys who hadn't started to shave yet, not for hairy adults. And if you liked to have a puff with your pals, far be it from Marguerite to stop you.

Later, as the serpent buried its fangs more deeply into us, we'd have whip-rounds and the same older-looking desperado would enter the shop and buy five Woodbine cigarettes for nine old pennies.

If you'd asked me at that time what the appeal was, I'd have told you that I took up smoking regularly in deference to approaching manhood.

No cat burglar from the kind of detective fiction I used to devour around sixty-odd years ago moved more stealthily than thirteen year old Tormod on that red-letter Saturday morning in 1950. Though I was in my own house in 191 Brand Street, I glided silently on stockinged feet from the back bedroom I shared with my mother's brother, *Cailean Beag*, Wee Colin MacKinnon, into the lobby hallway which separated bedroom and bathroom from the kitchen with its recessed bed, fireplace, cooker and sink. The kitchen was the living room and nerve centre of the Maclean household, five souls, at that time. Through the partially open kitchen door I could hear the low rumble of conversation between my father, *Niall Mòr*, Big Neil, and my mother, *Peigi Bheag*. Occasionally I detected a high-pitched interjection from my six year old sister, Lorna Flora.

Good. Wee Colin hadn't yet returned from the football match at Ibrox Park, and the coast was clear for a couple of minutes at least. Slowly, slowly, I inserted forefinger and thumb into the outside pocket of my father's donkey-jacket which hung on a hook above the coal box. For all my tender years I had a massive nicotine habit, and I was searching for the square packet of 'Capstan' cigarettes my father was never without. With my blood flowing red, I extracted the sky-blue coloured cigarette packet and as I fumbled with the silver foil enclosing the smooth, white tubes of my addiction I tried to ignore the trembling of my fingers. I stole only a single cigarette from the fifteen or so in the packet. My father wouldn't miss one, I hoped. It was when I was

115

replacing the 'Capstan' packet I felt a crumpled sheet of glossy paper which I transferred smoothly to the hip pocket of my short trousers. I'm aware that confessing to wearing short trousers when I was thirteen makes me rather quaint. But back in the day, boys didn't get to wear 'longies' until they were at least fourteen.

Thirty-seven seconds after I had swiped the cigarette, I was crouched on the front steps of our close examining this flyer that my father had inexplicably kept in the pocket of his working gear. The document proclaimed in bold red upper case letters: MORAL RE-ARMAMENT. Now, at that time I was a chain-reader, a paid-up member of a private lending library called the Grosvenor on Paisley Road West. Although I sucked voraciously at any printed material I could get my hands on, my reading never achieved any depth. It was all Bang! Bang! Bang! Hurry! Hurry! Hurry! The driblets of juice I extracted from the MRA pamphlet, as I recall them today, were disjointed and naïve. The phrases included: '… international moral and spiritual movement …Christian roots …Oxford Group … headquarters in Caux sur Montreux in Switzerland … core idea – changing the world starts with seeking change in oneself … absolute moral values of honesty, purity, unselfishness and love …'

Immediately I handed a metaphoric Rejection Slip to this piece of pie-in-the-sky prose. What a bunch of weirdos! I pegged the exalted initiatives of these deluded pioneers of an ideology inspired by God as the ravings of embarrassing oldsters. A disbelieving snort of mocking laughter issued from my nostrils as I read that all peoples could unite – Catholic, Jew, Protestant, Hindu, Muslim, Buddhist and Confucianist – in adherence to this squeaky-clean creed. These people, I thought at the time, have committed themselves to a set of absurd attitudes that were diametrically opposed to those embraced by the majority of folk within my ken. We, who were undergoing 'education', knew that the unbridled capitalistic world we would inherit was a rough place. Why did these wishy-washy idealists ignore the wealth-creating powers of the global market? Absolute honesty and purity and all that great-sounding stuff? Gimme a break. Absolute unselfishness and love? Didn't they know that corruption was endemic in capitalism and that Darwin himself had acknowledged it was a dog-eat-dog world out there? Love between the Catholic Fitzsimmon gang of rabid Celtic supporters and the Protestant Johnny Walker loyalist tribe of Rangers fans? Puh-leeeze.

This is what I think. Right enough, I am only thirteen at the time, but *Niall Mòr*, my father, hasn't bought into the values of MRA, has he? As a matter of fact, he has … slightly. He has taken a tiny glamhach, nibble at the agenda of the Moral Re-Armament movement. I think he just fancies a trip to Caux and wants to increase his chances of being a member of a delegation of trade unionists from Clydeside who are about to be invited to attend an indoctrination course in Switzerland in the month of October.

One Sunday afternoon, about a week after purloing the cigarette, my father stunned me. As usual he is attempting to tidy up copies of the Sunday Post and the News of the World from the faded carpet.

"Norman?" he says.

"Yes?"

"Put that book down and pay attention," he snaps. It was a novel called The Devil Rides Out by Denis Wheatley. "We're keeping you off the school tomorrow. Your mother'll write you a note on Tuesday morning."

"Okay … that's … I mean," I stammer. "But why … I mean, what's the reason for getting of school? What am I supposed to be …you know, doing tomorrow?"

"You're coming up the town with me and Matt Byrne, and you'll bring your pipes with you, tuigsinn, understand?"

I don't really. But I do know that Matt Byrne is the chairman of the Walmer Crescent-based branch of the Transport and General Workers' Union, the TGWU, where my father is part-time secretary. Matt Byrne's disdain for hard graft of any kind, especially back-breaking work that involves being trapped in the dusty holds of cargo ships hauling two hundredweight grain sacks to net slings made of rope which, when full, will be winched up on to the dock-side, is exceeded only by his passive affection for pints of draught Guinness in pubs in the Govan Road like The Kyles Of Bute and The Chevalier. I like to think my father was elected to the post of secretary because, not only is he smart, but he is also the possessor of beautiful copperplate handwriting.

With hindsight and with increasing personal decrepitude caused by advancing years, I suspect he was worn out by the favouritism and corruption of the daily 'line-up' at the dock gates and was keen to take up a softer and more sedentary occupation. The old man wanted to sling the docker's hook and the moleskin trousers and swap them for the sober suit, collar and tie and soft hat of a sedentary office worker.

"What are we going up the town for?" I say.

"You're to pipe the arrival of the London night train at the Central."

"Play the pipes in Central Station?" I gasp. "Why?"

"Because the Govan branch of the TGWU are welcoming a very important member of the Moral Re-Armament movement," Big Neil replies.

"Who's that?" I enquire aware that this visitor must be some kind of a gigantic deal before my parents will allow me to be absent from school for a whole day. Most Highland parents revere education for their offspring and none more so than *Niall Mòr* and *Peigi Bheag*.

"Lady Norah Docker," my father announces smugly.

It takes but a second or two to recall the images from

newspapers and Pathe News. I see in a kind of black and white show reel pictures of a tall, glamorous lady invariably dressed in figure-hugging ball gown beneath a fur outer garment. My father explained that Lady Docker had started off her glittering career of conspicuous consumption as a dance-hostess in London's Café de Paris, and had married three times, on each occasion to an executive of a business that sold luxury goods. Her third marriage, to Sir Bernard Docker, Chairman of Birmingham Small Arms and its subsidiary the Daimler Motor Company, was notable for the couple's flamboyant, excessive behaviour. It was clear that this formidable lady had worked hard to enjoy easy money. Shìorraidh, Goodness, I am about to be thrust into broilleach nan uaislean, the bosom of the gentility.

Monday morning, twenty past eight, bagpipes on my shoulder, I am marching in full Highland day-dress – navy Balmoral bonnet with red 'toorie' on top, short bright green tweed jacket, MacLean tartan kilt, knee high Lovat stockings and highly polished black brogues – back and forth, fifteen feet along Platform One in Central station towards a slowly approaching steam train. I march in sprightly fashion towards it. I decide to make a slow, careful turn. I set off again for another fifteen feet in the opposite direction, prancing on the balls of my feet and all the while battering out 'Step We Gaily', 'High Road to Gairloch' and 'Brown Haired Maiden' on my brand new Grainger and Campbell bagpipe. (Today I recall with a pang of guilt that my father had paid old Campbell in his cramped booth in a pen-close in Argyle Street thirty-five pounds for this instrument – the equivalent of ten weeks net pay back then. This was quite a commitment from a dock labourer to his only son).

'Brown Haired Maiden' isn't particularly apposite as a salute to Lady Docker. She has long since ceased to be a maiden and her hair is pineapple blonde. She is tall, in a short striped coat made from the skin of some animal. Almost horizontal dark eyebrows frame blue eyes. The heavily powdered face is dominated by a rather broad straight nose and an over-wide, carmine-red mouth with a full lower lip.

She is smiling at an old porter who has been carefully pushing a trolley heaped with leather suitcases behind her swivelling hips as she sashays like some cat-walk model down the length of the platform. She presses something into his hand and with an imperious wave of her arm despatches the serge-clad ancient in the direction of the Central Hotel at the far end of the concourse. With an even wider friendly smile she shakes hands with Matt Byrne and my father. I take this as a cue to conclude my bagpipe recital and with many a flourish and with much twirling of drones and chanter I assume the at-ease position. I feel like *Mac Iain 'ic Sheumais* coming into Carinish, North Uist to vanquish the MacLeods in *Teampall na Trianaid*, the Temple of the Trinity.

Lady Docker, arm in arm with *Niall Mòr* and with Matt Byrne in tow, approaches me. My father places his extra large hand on top of my red 'toorie' and says simply: "Lady Docker – *Lettie Daaw-ch-ker* – this is my son – *sih-in*."

Part of me is pleased that my father seems to be proud of me. Part of me cringes at his heavy Hebridean accent. The lady directs her painted smile towards me, looks me right in the eye, extends her hand and says, "What's your name, little boy?"

I open my mouth, but I am already intimidated and nothing comes out.

"Oh," my father says, "he's called Norman … Hector … MacKinnon … Maclean." Aw, no! How could you do this to me?

"What a big name for such a little boy!" Lady Docker says.

I catch a whiff of condescension. "Mah frien's ca' me Norrie," I say. For anyone of an imitative nature, and I was certainly of that tribe, it is a doddle to drift into the Govan way of saying things.

"No, I prefer Norman Hector –*Naaw-min Heck-tah*," she flutes. "Now, shall we knock the introductions on the head? I want a quick bite to eat – *hello-oh*? – and, as I remember, there's a little sea-food restaurant in town called the Rogano that's passable. We could have a spot of kedgeree there."

Matt Byrne gives my father an anxious glance, and I immediately know that the tribunes of the Govan Branch of the TGWU can't afford the prices in a mysterious restaurant up the town and that, moreover, they haven't a scoobie as to what kedgeree is. The truth is that, between us, Matt, Big Neil and me, we know as much about fine dining as we do about nuclear physics.

Matt Byrne pipes up: "Hey, Missus Docker, Luigi's Caff is jist roon the coarner, under the Hielanman's Umbrella. He serves a rare – *rerr* – breakfast."

"That's right," my father adds rapidly. "I had the egg and chips there one time – *wan toime* – and it was really – *ree-ally* – good."

The Hielanman's Umbrella, a nickname that is still used to this day, was coined in the early 20th century. Gaelic-speaking Highlanders who were sweeping into the city in great numbers then would often meet under the railway bridge which crossed Argyle Street as it entered the Central Station. There, at the *Drochaid*, Bridge, they sheltered from the rain, met male and female members of their ethnic group and, in today's parlance, generally hung out.

A silence. Then Lady Docker smiles patiently and says, "All right let's all go to Luigi's Caff." She remembers something. "Is it far?"

"Five minutes' walk," *Niall Mòr* offers.

"Wish I'd had one of the Daimlers driven up," says the lady.

CAFÉ DE PARIS MEETS THE HIELANMAN'S UMBRELLA

Our table in the service section of Luigi's Caff, well to the rear of the counter by the doorway, has a slick bright orange vinyl laminate top on which rests a nest of condiments and a single stained menu. On the walls on either side are alarmingly detailed blown-up framed photographs of the house specials. These include giant-sized plates with huge chunks of yellow battered cod surrounded by heaps of dark brown re-heated chips, cremated rashers of bacon topped by the oozing yokes of fried eggs and circled by a deep ring of French fries. There are also massive images of greasy circular slices of blood pudding beneath a thick mantle of melted cheese with side portions of buttered bread and fried potato scones dripping with grease.

Unsurprisingly, we have the sitting room to ourselves. Lady Docker, seated next to my father, opposite me and Mr Byrne, swings her head round from wall to wall, makes a *eeeeyuk* face and says rather hopefully, "Looks very quiet, doesn't it? Maybe we should try somewhere else."

"Naw, ye're a' right, hen," Mr Byrne says soothingly. "The lassie'll be oot any minute noo." He offers the menu with the congealed stains of tomato ketchup on it to her. "Whit dae ye fancy?"

Lady Docker holds the menu between thumb and forefinger, the way you might transport a dead seagull on the Uist machair by the tip of one wing. She looks at the offending object as if it has just crawled up her leg. "Hmmm," she says, cocking her head in a way that makes me feel uneasy. I know that this repast will be the most embarrassing of my short life.

Matt Byrne starts it all off by asking Lady Docker what kind of work her 'man' (husband) does.

"Well," says Lady Docker with a fling of a bejewelled hand and an ingratiating smile, "He's in ...you know, it's hard for me to answer that question accurately ....he's involved in engineering in Birmingham."

"He's an engineer?" Byrne says. "That's a rare – *rerr* – number, so it is."

Part of me cringes. I know that whatever Sir Bernard Docker does to earn a crust, he will have nothing in common with the journeymen and their apprentices who at lunch time every day pour out in waves from every shipyard that lines the Govan Road. These troglodytes in their shiny blue overalls and with their grease-stained faces are known as 'engineers' but I doubt they and Bernie were brothers under the skin.

A smile of tried patience from the lady: "No, he's the Chief Executive Officer of Birmingham Small Arms – BSA, you understand."

"Oh, I've heard of them," old Matt blurts out.

So have I: indeed, I covet the 125cc model of the famous motorbike manufactured by that company. I have no great confidence, however, I'll be able to afford the asking price on my earnings from my milk run. I also have a general idea what a chief executive officer is, and I knew the Dockers are too rich for my peasant blood.

To rescue a drowning moment, I whisper, "Excuse me, Lady Docker, but do you possess a BSA motorcycle?"

From the lady's throat there issues a stagey laugh. She glances at my father and Mr Byrne and then she says to me: "Actually, no, Norman Hector. But I am having a special gold-plated Daimler car built for me."

"A Daimler?" my father gasps with reverence in his voice, and I remember that, according to my mother, Big Neil had once owned an Austin Seven saloon long before I put in an appearance.

"Yes," says Lady Docker, placing her hand on his forearm and giving it a slight squeeze. "You see, Sir Bernard is …like … chairman of BSA's subsidiary, the Daimler Motor Company. And they're having a touring limousine made especially for me. When it's finished it'll be covered with 7,000 tiny gold stars and all the plating …in normal cars it'd be chrome …in my car it'll be in pure gold."

The three of us gaze at her with awe and even a degree of disbelief.

"But what do you do, Lady (Letty)?" my father asks in a low pitched voice. "What do you make? What do you sell? What do you serve to people? You understand me? What is your job?"

Lady Docker turns to Daddy and her mouth shimmies into a sickening grin. "Tell me, Mr Maclean, what do you do?"

"Me?" my father gamely replies. "Well, I work – wirrk – at the King George Vth dock in Shieldhall, KGV?" He looks directly into her eyes. "I used to be a bosun with Donaldson Line, mainly Glasgow to St Johns, some trips to India, but mainly Glasgow to North – Norse – America – Amaireeka."

Lady Docker favours him with an even broader smile. "Oh, you're a seafaring man," she trills. "How thrilling! You'll have to come for a sail on our yacht, the Shemara, next time we come up to Scotland." She takes daddy's hand and says, "Mr Maclean …" with a deep look into the eyes and an inflection that bespeaks a sympathetic confidentiality. "Don't you just adore Monaco?"

It seems to me that Big Neil looks at Lady Docker a couple of beats longer than is necessary before saying lightly, "I can't say I ever – *effer* – had the pleasure of putting in – *een* – at that place, ma'am."

To this very day I can hear her voice, laden with insincerity and I can see the curling of her upper lip, the mischievous gleam of the nouvelle arriviste in her eye.

Imagine the dinner scene on the previous evening in their Hampshire estate. This trip, as she would have explained to Sir Bernard, was the very last thing she needed just now. She couldn't wait for it to be over. But there was no getting out of it, darling. The people in Caux were depending on her. These dock labourers in Glasgow had to be vetted for their suitability for the introductory autumn MRA training course in Switzerland. She had to mix with these people, dine with them – some shanty Irishman called Byrne and his sidekick, Neil Macsomethingorother – engage in hollow chit-chat with them. She hated having conversations with people whose accents she couldn't penetrate. She'd just have to grin like an idiot at the guttural accents of these … oiks. If there was such a thing as a working telephone in this slum called Glasgow, she'd try to call. But realistically, darling, she was afraid that she wouldn't be able to get in touch for a day or two.

After considerable study, Lady Docker, here in Luigi's Caff, orders fried chicken with chips, baked beans and deep-fried onion rings. There is scarcely any delay between placing our orders with the middle-aged lady in the grubby overall and the arrival of the dishes. And each dish is … big. Each plate is laden with deep fried food. Big Neil launches into his tennis-racket sized haddock and chips with obvious appetite. Matt and I have about seven pounds of thick-cut French fries each, along with pint glasses of American Cream Soda. Lady Docker studies her fried chicken as if it was a sleeping animal. She doesn't smile and speaks not.

We, the Glasgow contingent, bolt down our portions. From Lady Docker's plate only one thing has disappeared – a morsel of chicken breast about the size of a two shilling bit, from where she has peeled back the fried skin.

"That's whit ah tellt ye, missus, so ah did," Matt Byrne splutters through a mouthful of chips. "Ye willnae leave Luigi's hungry, eh?"

Old Norah Docker, former dance hostess in London's Café de Paris, has no response to Matt Byrne's remark except to nod half a dozen times while chewing very, very slowly.

The jolly baritone of Daddy as he beams at everyone breaks the silence. "Well, what do you all think – *seenk*? Plenty of good food here, eh?"

Daddy chews down on the last forkful of haddock and announces, "Matt, I was wondering if I should go back to the office this afternoon …you know, instead of going back to the 'Control' to see if the ganger has a shift – *sheeft* – for me. What do you think – *sink*?"

Matt glances at Daddy. Then he says to Lady Docker, "Don't know whit the Govan Branch of the TGWU wid dae wi'oot Big Neil here. We're a' real proud o' him."

Lady Docker cocks her head and stares at Daddy. Daddy smiles modestly and shrugs his broad shoulders. "I'm sure," Lady Docker says with the fake bonhomie she has learned to exercise when forced to confront plebs, "Mr Maclean is worthy of all praise." She consults her platinum Rolex importantly, as if she expects a terrorist bomb to go off at any moment. "Tell you what, I'll keep you in mind, Neil, if anything comes up at our end, and I promise to …keep …in …touch." She shakes Daddy's hand and then puts her other hand on top of his, making a warm sandwich.

"That's very civil – *ceeffil* – of you, ma'am," Big Neil says. "You see, I'm sick of working – *wirrking* – in the holds of grain boats and iron ore ships. I want to become a respectable man."

"Most commendable, sir," Lady Docker says, turning on her most encouraging smile yet.

"Yes," Daddy continues, almost recklessly, "if I can replace the moleskin trouser (this article of men's clothing is always singular among Gaelic speakers) with a smart three-piece suit and a desk job in a warm, cosy office ... I would not wish – *weesh* – to leave this world."

Lady Docker takes a very long time to arrange her cutlery on top of an oozing mound of fried food. She makes a eeeeyuk face as if she wants to vomit.

I barely notice. A single Gaelic locution imported in its entirety into the English language, would not wish to leave this world, has delivered a mighty punch to my solar plexus – to me, a young blade absolutely dripping with promise.

No, my father has crossed the line here. It is the poverty of ambition in his dreams for the future that causes my cheeks to turn crimson. I am different, I assure myself. While it seems unlikely that my father will let me go to sea, as I yearn to do, — "Never, *a Thormoid*, lift anything heavier than a bar of chocolate or a pen when you grow up." — I know, deep down, I will move erratically on the winds of rumour and opportunity all over Europe, North and South America, with forays to the Far East. I'll jump from one country to another, always looking for the big break, the crucial job interview, the rich patron, even the blonde nymphomaniac Swedish heiress at the end of every train journey or airline flight.

A little later on, Lady Docker yawns without covering her open mouth. "Oh, I'm so tired," she says. "Hardly slept at all last night down in Hampshire. It's always the same. I hardly close an eyelid the night before I'm off somewhere. Especially when I'm travelling to somewhere ... exciting." This lie is delivered in a voice that is resonant of post-war Berlin, or even the Café de Paris, at a stretch, the kind of voice that filters well through cigarette smoke. As an actress, I divine, Norah Docker was no Marlene Dietrich. She turns to me.

"And how did you sleep, little man?"

"I don't know, I was asleep."

In addition to everything else, almost great piper, low-echelon boxer, middling classical scholar, I am a notorious comedian.

Nobody finds my line amusing and once Lady Docker has departed for her suite in the Central Hotel at the corner of Hope Street and Gordon Street, my father, Byrne and I were ambling down Jamaica Street. Halfway between Argyle Street and the Broomielaw we came to a halt and my father crouched down and placed his extra large hand round the nape of my neck and pulled me close to whisper in my ear. "*A Thormoid*, Norman," he hissed in Gaelic, "apart from that crack about not knowing how you slept last night, you behaved very well in the company of that lady who says she'll maybe do your father a bit of good." He made a derisory snorting noise. "*Na creid facal dheth*, Don't believe a word of it. As the old proverb has it '*is sleamhainn ursainn an taighe mhòir*, slippery indeed is the threshold of the big house.' Don't rely on another person to be your advocate. *Cuimhnich an còmhnaidh air na daoine bhon tàini*' thu, always remember the people from whom you're descended. Though you're here in Mighty Glasgow of the marble pavilions, you're only passing through. '*S e eileanach a th' annad*, you're an islander, and you'll endure." He went into his trouser pocket and took out a shilling. "Here," he said, wrapping my fingers round the coin, "*Thalla air ais dhan sgoil a-nis*, Off you go back to school now. Me and Matt are nipping into McSorley's for a quick dram."

The pair of them walked through the arched entrance to the public house, chatting away as I crossed Jamaica Street to the tram stop and boarded a number 40 tramcar.

DEATH OF A FATHER

I, fourteen, on a bitterly cold Sunday afternoon in early December, tell the girl in the tightly belted green raincoat, I'll meet her at the Art Galleries in a week's time. We are standing in a lane behind Partick Cross Underground station (renamed Kelvinhall) face to face, her arms round my waist, mine resting lightly on her shoulders. "I'll see you at the same time in the same place. You know, in front of Salvador Dali's Crucifixion'?'"

"You're not going to be seeing me again, Norman," says this young girl from Finnieston who, like me, is a third year pupil in a Secondary School in the city. She attends Woodside on the north bank of the Clyde, while I am displaying a lot of promise in Bellahouston Academy on the south side . I see in her eyes the desperate longing I was to see many times in the future.

"I'll do my best," I lie. I remove my hands from her shoulders and place them in the safety of my trouser pockets. "Look, I've got to trap," I mumble. "It's Sunday night on the Underground, and my old man'll be home from the King George V dock by now ...and I've got a Latin Ink Exercise to do for school tomorrow."

I cannot leave it like that. I have to finish with a few untruths. "I'll see you next week at the Art Galleries, all right?" I say, knowing it was all wrong.

There is a silence between us for two or three seconds. We both seek the hem of our stories: the clean parting, and the separation is cloying, without satisfaction.

Half an hour later I leave Copland Road (re-named Ibrox) Underground Station and stride proudly up Woodville Street and on to Brand Street. At the close entrance our next door neighbour, Mr Bankhead, a rigger from Belfast, places his hand on my chest as I try to wriggle past him.

"I'd like a word with you, Norman," he says quietly.

"I've got to get up the stairs, Mr Bankhead."

"Not right away, son," he says in the lengthened and flattened vowels of Ulster. "Yer ma asked me speak to ye."

"So?" I say.

"Yer da's had an accident down at KG Five, son,"he announces solemnly.

"What kind of accident – what do you mean, Mr Bankhead?" I say, a

shrillness creeping into my voice.

"He's dead, Norman," Bankhead says in funereal tones.

"Where is he?" I enquire.

"He's up the stair," Bankhead says. "Yer ma's with the body. Yer wee sister's in with us and the boys."

"I'd better go, Mr Bankhead," I say hurriedly.

"Be good to yer ma, son," Mr Bankhead says softly.

Getting to the heart of the day my daddy died, I'm almost overcome by the emotions of shame and guilt on my part and the mystery almost revealed by Big Neil earlier that Sunday morning.

At around eleven thirty our entire family – mother, father, my young sister Lorna and myself – are together in the kitchen of our 'hoose.' This will be the last day in the life of *Niall Mòr*. I am seated at the table, my back to the window, drinking tea. I've given up attending

Sunday School at St Columba's, Copland Road for about six months now, pleading tiredness after activity-filled evenings at the Saturday night BB club. My mother is washing up behind me at the sink. Lorna Flora is playing with her dolls on the recessed bed and my father is crouched in the big chair by the fireplace trying to reassemble the jumbled pages of the Sunday Post that I have scattered carelessly on the floor after reading them earlier. My wee Uncle Colin is spending the weekend with his cousin Willie Macdonald (*Uilleam Alasdair 'ic Aonghais 'ic Iain Mhòir*) in Falkirk. My father is wearing brown moleskin trousers and heavy brown boots, stained by iron ore dust. He will be off shortly to work at unloading a Canadian grain boat moored down at the King George v dock in Shieldhall. He's in a bad mood.

"Norman," says my father in English, "why can't you learn yourself to put a newspaper back the way you found it?"

"Daddy," I reply, and when I recall my sarcasm, a tide of filthy water scalds my throat, "if you insist on speaking a language whose grammar will always be problematic to you, please remember that the verb 'learn' is inappropriate before a personal pronoun: 'teach' is the word you should have used."

The big man is speechless.

These are the last words I will speak to my father while he is still alive.

"*Cuine thilleas tu an-nochd*, When will you be back tonight?" *Peigi Bheag* enquires of her husband.

"*Cò aig tha brath*, Who knows?" my father replies. "*B' shuarach orm an obair seo a dhiùltadh gu glan, mas e seo an taing tha mi a' faighinn*, It wouldn't take much for me to turn down the shift completely, if this is the kind of thanks I'm getting."

"*Cia air a bhitheamaid beò an uairsin*, What would we live on then?"

"*Air ùrlar bhur sgamhan 's dòcha*, On the bottom of your lungs perhaps."

My mother steps away from the sink, drying her hands on a towel, and walks over to the big chair. "*Cha ruigeadh tu leas a bhith a' dèanamh do chosnaidh an grùnnd ifhreann mar seo*, You didn't have to be earning a living in the depths of hell like this." But why did my father leave an important, well-paid job as shore bosun with the Donaldson Line Shipping Company and become a poorly paid dock labourer?

"*Tha fhios agad mar a chaill mi an obair aig Donaldson*, You know how I lost the job with Donaldson?"

"*Tha*, Yes."

"*Uill, leig as t' inntinn e*, Well, just forget it."

Mura b'e na 'Lascars,' dh' fhaodamaid a bhith seasgair, tèarmainnaichte, blàth ann am 'bungalow' *ann an Ralston an-dràsta, seach a bhith beò air a' bhochdainn an sheo ann am* Brand Street, If it hadn't been for the 'Lascars,' we could be sitting snug, cosy and warm in a bungalow in Ralston just now, rather than barely surviving in poverty here in Brand Street." Golly! Lascars! This is better than any of the mysteries Valentine Dial broadcasts on the wireless.

"*Reic thu cuidheall ròpa nach b' fhiach am poll ris na h-Innseanaich, chaidh an glacadh leis na poileis shuas am baile is dh' innis iad-san ort*, You sold a coil of rope worth very little to the Indians, they were caught by the police up the town and they told on you," my mother announces triumphantly.

My father remains silent for a good two minutes, then clumps heavily out of his room and kitchen home. *Co chreideadh e*, Who'd believe it? My father is a thief! Is that why he reacts so badly to my delinquency? Does he see something of himself in me?

I turns out that after my priggish lecture on English usage at noon, my father, accompanied by two teuchter fellow-dockers, suffers a massive heart attack. He is brought by taxi – a Mr Campbell, a native of Lewis, organised this – to the Co-operative

Funeral Home in Nelson Street, Kingston. The undertaker does his stuff and returns to our home with the coffin in late afternoon.

None of what follows – the casket in the middle of the back room where Colin and I sleep fitfully in the recessed double bed, the three days and nights of psalm singing, the terror of sharing a room with a corpse — was a dream, but it passed like a dream.

At the funeral service in the same room three days later I kiss my father's brow. I am astonished at the coldness of his skin and how hard the bone beneath it is.

As I look down at his chalk-white face I kind of understand my father's desire to abandon a life of unremitting physical toil for something a wee bit cushier. Oh, sure, the poor guy gets to go to Caux sur Montreux, but fourteen months later he is dead. I remember Big Neil's hammering Lady Norah Docker about what kind of work she did, and an irony hits me. Neil couldn't find a job that would improve the lot of himself and his family, and old Norah didn't need one. They had something in common! I don't know if Lord and Lady Docker really intended to be his patrons. Somehow I don't think so. He never did get to wear a suit and work in a warm office. Though he didn't wish it, he left this world far too early.

Me? My overwhelming emotions at my father's death are shame and a resentment that gradually turns to anger. On the day of his burial in Cardonald cemetery I abruptly became the man of the house. This is a role I am too young to assume. The fact that I am now eligible for free school meals and have to receive a 'special' Dinner Ticket every Monday morning means that my classmates are completely separated from me. Every time our form master hands me my buff-coloured ticket such is my sense of shame that I imagine my heartbeat is audible to the entire class.

Oh, I rejoice in the freedom given to me by my overworked mother - the key of the door and the right to come and go as I please - but there are little signs I perceive only dimly, without understanding, that hint at unimagined possibilities attached to breaking loose from my father's strict discipline.

At the age of fourteen I embark on a career of conscientious hedonism. It is clear now that what I have been looking for my entire life is the main chance: the shortcut no one else had seen. I become a drifter, a malcontent, a stupid drunk who never loses the conviction that somehow inevitably I'll make it to the summit of the mountain. I have convinced myself that I am a person of hidden or soon–to-be-revealed virtue.

One of the benefits of Big Neil's premature death is that I no longer have to worry about the 'Mrs Bryson issue.' My father has been unhappy with his marriage for a long time and our regular 'Sunday treat' with the elegant blonde woman whose husband was an accompanist at the BBC in Queen Margaret Drive has been a constant guilty memory and is now terminated.

But the emotion within me is boiling anger. As a dutiful son I wear the black cloth diamond of mourning on the sleeves of every outer garment I possess. I go from white plimsoles or 'sannies' to black socks with suspenders round the calf overnight. I accept that I cannot attend the Third Year Christmas Dance with apparent equanimity, but this filial piety is feigned. Away from home, I become an actor, concealing my anger and underlying general sense of unease by adopting a reckless, devil-may-care persona. Sometimes, however, the mask slips and loathing and madness boil over. From time to time I rail against the fact that I am now the man of the house. I direct my anger not against my father, but against God. On one occasion in the middle of a hailstorm as I am returning from a football match at Ibrox Park I am assaulted by waves of fear and loathing. I detach myself from the little clump of Rangers supporters who have surrounded me since the end of the match. I shelter in the first close on Paisley

Road West after Whitefield Road. I now see it all very clearly. I shake my fist up at the grey, hail-filled sky where God resides. Where is my minister when I need him? Lord, my dad was not guilty. I am guilty. I reject you and all you stand for. All Big Neil did was take your gibberish seriously …and I see where that got him. This is your work, Lord! I'll take care of myself from now on, thanks, and if I don't, you can bring down the hammer any time you like.

From the first year of mourning for my father there is a long-lost echo of a strange event that occurred on an afternoon excursion to the coastal town of Largs. My mother is seriously strapped for money now and the only summer break she can afford to give to me and Lorna is a run in the top deck of a bus, in all its bright yellow and cream livery, which plies its way twice daily between the city and the Ayrshire holiday resort.

A circuit round the bay in an open decked speedboat follows the obligatory purchase of ice cream cones in Nardini's. In the middle of the bay we see an upturned rowing boat, no sign of any oars, and close by, the heads of two men bobbing above the water. They appear to be fighting! They exchange punches until one of the crewmen on our vessel throws life-belts in their direction. They grab hold of them and are hoisted aboard our boat where they collapse, hair, faces and good suits dripping wet, into the bilges.

"*Dè thachair*, What happened?" I ask my mother.

"*Tud, chan eil orra ach an daorach, Och*, that's just drunkenness," she says dismissively.

BOOM. I remember I'm a soldier at war with the Almighty. Drunkenness? I haven't really started yet, mother, but when I do, I'll give you drunkenness all right.

And that's exactly what I did. The poor woman spent her life savings on getting me admitted for detox in the Crichton Royal and 'cures' in expensive gaffs like the Priory.

For a long time I attributed the nightmare of the next sixty years to an irresponsible Creator. Some fool in Heaven, by taking my daddy away from me before I was ready, did this to me. It was *your* idea, Lord, not mine.

****

I know that there was always something wrong in the way my father related to me, but my thinking on this has always been a bit fuzzy. I am still asking myself who he really was as Big Neil never revealed his scars to the crowd as Corialanus did.

Rereading accounts of my father's punitive excesses seventy years on I am aware that readers may think that my father's disproportionate punishment constituted child abuse. *Feumaidh mi solas eile a chur air a'ghnothach*, I'll have to cast a different light on the matter. I certainly knew from comparing crimes and punishments with other kids that my dad's discipline was a tad rigid. But I also knew something else, even while he was administering his version of appropriate justice. I knew that with every crack of the belt or the broad palm of his hand on my bare buttocks and lower back Big Neil was beating something out of himself.

I've been rooting around in my mental attic for the origins of my inability to judge risks and to regulate my behaviour, once I had embarked on a particular course of action. When I'd start to drink, for example, I'd keep on doing it even as I realised that the action was destroying my life. The obtrusive thought would be: well, Norman, you've now knackered the contract. You're back on the downward spiral. You may as well carry on indefinitely. I guess that my father was damaged too, and while he would try to eschew violent behaviour for long periods, troubling memories would be dredged from time to time, and he would succumb to the temptation to take his latent anger out on his only son.

I wasn't always as magnanimous as this. When they clothed him in his best and only suit and placed him in the box I was assailed in equal measure by resentment and sadness. Over sixty years have passed and I've turned the page on my earlier interpretation.

From repeated accusations against my dad made by his younger brother Hugh Maclean, and little parenthetical asides from my mother, I learned that Big Neil Maclean did not have a good time in this world. Uncle Hughie, particularly if he was in his cups, always accused my father of breaking his mother's heart when he left the family home in 'The Green' on Tiree to join the crew of a Dutch sailing vessel at the age of fourteen. "*Thug thu bàs ealamh dhi*, You brought her to an early death," the man with the biggest hands in Christendom would intone sorrowfully with a drudging plough-horse devotion to endless repetition. His brother's charges did have an effect on my father. I could see Neil's emotions were balanced on the fulcrum between anger and anguish. I venture to suggest, too, that guilt over the theft of rope from Donaldson's stores, an indiscreet admission by my mother, played a part in ratcheting up his aggression towards me.

Today, I'm free to speculate on what was going on with my father when guilt and an abhorrence of theft led him to react in such a violent way. Now that I'm no longer afraid to let fuzzy thought from the past into the forefront of my brain I've come to the conclusion that his cerebral processes were not all that different from my own. Like me, he set himself high standards, and when, in the natural order of things, he failed to meet them, he sought relief by losing himself in a self-harming spiral.

My Creator has forgiven my trespasses. It's only fitting that I should forgive my father's trespasses against me.

CHASING THE LOWEY

Anyone who happened to be lolling against the side door of Montgomery's Licensed Grocers at the corner of Paisley Road West and Elizabeth Street round about six o'clock on a cold, damp February morning in 1952 would have been nonplussed by a mysterious blinding flash created by a dashing stripling who was indistinguishable from the present writer at the age of fifteen. The protagonist in this little evocation of mid-century hardship in the second city of the Empire was descended from a race of Hebridean kings. Yes, it was I, who streaked two blocks down Elizabeth Street on that damp morning so many years ago.

The idler would have seen the blur of a puny figure, dressed in off-white singlet, khaki shorts and white plimsoles or, as the Americans say, sneakers. The plimsolls or 'sannies', short for 'sand shoes', were liberally coated with white 'blanco' every night before retiral, and if it were raining the following day, every time the milkboy came to a squelching halt, the 'blanco' combined with the rain water to produce a thin trickle of grey excrescence which briefly stained the pavement. At incalculable speed this rapid stripling, head lowered to reduce wind resistance, streaked northwards up Elizabeth Street while propelling before him on outstretched arms a two-wheeled barrow. The barrow, or 'barra' as it was known locally, was composed of tubular steel, had big fat tires and was loaded with three crates of milk bottles, say sixty pints in total. So swift had been the stripling's speed that it was only when he and his 'barra' had skidded to a halt at the entrance to the close numbered nineteen in the red sandstone tenement that the identity of the fifteen year old sprinter could be confirmed. A third year student of Latin and French at Bellahouston Academy, this Gaelic speaking Govanite was going places, fast. At this point in time he was going up the stairs at number nineteen, taking them three at a time, with six – I repeat, six! – pint bottles of milk. He had three bottles distributed among the outspread fingers of each hand, and he knew exactly beside which doors he had to place one bottle of full cream or two pints of regular or whatever the householder had ordered. Empty bottles, a single beside Mrs Docherty's front door on the first landing, a couple of pairs at the doors of Anderson and Clarke who were two-up, and another single at the door of old Mr Brechin on the top landing confirmed that these folk were indeed his customers. Quickly snatching up old Brechin's smelly bottle – the oldster never rinsed the pint bottle when he'd emptied it – our milkboy would bound down the stairs like a stag and transfer the empties from the second landing to their allocated spaces between thumbs, index fingers and middle fingers of each hand. One to go. Leaping from half-landing to the first storey, he scooped up Mrs Docherty's spotlessly clean and gleaming pint bottle between pinkie and annular finger and charged down the remaining stairs to the close and out to his trusty chariot. He dumped the empties into the crate he had broached with satisfying clanging noises. Next, with a smooth shimmy, he grasped the rubber insulated horizontal crossbar that connected the handles of the 'barra' and he was off. Head down, legs pumping furiously, he raced northward across Ibrox Street, swerved right at Middleton Street and came to a slithering halt at its junction with Harley Street.

Okay, I've parked my 'barra' at the corner of Harley Street and Middleton Street, loaded up with six bottles, sometimes fewer, and plunged into various tenement closes within a radius of thirty yards. Over the next twenty minutes or so, with a standard deviation of around five minutes to accommodate changing weather conditions or alterations to the order card, this was the hectic merry-go-round of my early morning activity. I'd sprint up Harley Street to Walmer Crescent, halt at Cessnock Street, deliver orders there and in Percy Street. Next, I'd make a dash to Clifford Street, all the time plunging into dark closes, some with hazardous spiral staircases, to deliver full pint bottles and collect empties. A quarter mile dash westward brought me to my final stop in Kirkwood Street. There the 'rake' or delivery run was completed and, blowing hard and soaked in perspiration, I'd gallop back with three crates full of empties to the Co-operative dairy which was the home base for about a dozen lads like myself. With cheeks like Pippins I would croak, "That's me"– gulp of air – "finished" – gulp of air – "first rake" – gulp of air – "a'right?" Then, unbelievably, I'd repeat the entire process: load up, grab a new order card, execute an explosive start, and embark on my second 'rake' of the day.

The reward for each 'rake' completed was ten old pennies. For delivering two 'rakes' each morning you earned one shilling and eight old pennies. When multiplied by the number of days in the week, the Co-op generously rounded up your weekly wage to twelve shillings, or sixty pence in today's currency. If you were feeling exceptionally fit, you might attempt three 'rakes' on a particular morning, say a Friday, to increase your daily wage to half a crown. The whole point of undertaking this back-breaking, lung-searing graft before returning home to change your clothing and wolf down a large breakfast consisting of porridge, boiled eggs and toast before heading off for school was to be in the position of proudly handing your mother twelve shillings every Saturday morning. Wee Peggy, *Peigi Anna Bige*, gave me back two shillings for pocket money and I was convinced she appreciated my weekly contribution to the family's finances. If she was happy, I was delighted, for I had access to another cash source.

Thanks to the goodwill of Angus John MacAulay from Baleshare, North Uist, and Calum MacLellan, *mac Eoghainn Bhig*, whose parents hailed from the west side of North Uist, I was offered a permanent gig as the piper at the weekly ceilidhs of the Uist and Barra Association which were held, bizarrely enough, in the Orange Halls in Lorne Street, Plantation. I say 'bizarrely' because around half the adult audience and perhaps an even greater proportion of the boys and girls who were perched on the edge of the platform, bare legs dangling as they faced the audience, were communicants at the Roman Catholic church of St Margaret's in Kinning Park just half a mile along the Paisley Road West to the east. These natives of South Uist, Eriskay and Barra resolutely ignored the giant print of William of Orange astride a white horse which hung from the far wall of the function room.

I wish to emphasise a particular mind-set that obtained among tenement teuchters in the great city of Glasgow, Protestant and Roman Catholic, sixty years ago. We were not all that interested in the rituals and the mutual sectarian hatred of the Lowlanders, 'Proddies' and 'Papes'. We, as nominal Christians, communicants or adherents, were aware that our Creator's house had many mansions. What we were at pains to underline was our *otherness* in relation to our Lowland neighbours, workmates and school chums with whom we interacted on a daily basis. If the committee of the Uist and Barra Association had decided to rent rooms in, say, a Sikh Temple, then that's where we would have gathered. Surroundings didn't matter as long we were able commune on a weekly basis with the voices of *Flòrag an Tàilleir*, Flora Macneil from Barra, Effie Maceachan, the MacIver brothers, Alex J. Macdonald, Paul MacInnes, *Uisdean Sheumais*, Hugh Matheson from Baleshare, Allan MacRitchie, Al MacRury, *an gille aig Anna Ceit Uilleim*, (in my opinion the best Gaelic singer ever to emerge from Benbecula) and a host of others who regularly attracted large audiences to the venue every Saturday night. And the Orange Halls wasn't the only attraction for the tenement teuchters. On the other side of the water there were the Knightswood Highlanders and the Overnewton Ceilidh, while in the Cardell Halls at Govan Cross on Thursday nights the Govan Ceilidh was going full swing.

In the Orange Hall, my piping duties were light: a brief burst on the bagpipe to open proceedings at the start of each half and that was about it. *Seumas a' Mhinisteir*, James Macdonald from Barra, the regular MC always ensured there was a fifteen minute interval in proceedings to enable many of the adult males to troop over the road to Howden's Bar in Brand Street for a quick 'refreshment'. For a total of about eight minutes playing of Marches, Strathspeys, Reels and Jigs I was rewarded with a crisp ten shilling note (50p), half of which I gave to my mother and the other half I added to my pocket money. Man, I was gold-plated.

Why then did I persist in subjecting myself to the daily helter-skelter of the milk runs? I suppose my motivation was a murky compound of 'becoming a real man', filial piety and a desire to bond with my Lowland peers. One thing to be said in favour of gripping six pint sized bottles of milk at a time and running up tenement stairs with them every morning in life was that the exercise fairly strengthened my fingers. When it came to releasing the Teuchter facet of my personality on a Saturday night on the Great Highland Bagpipe, metaphoric sparks fairly flew from my chanter.

PLAYTIME

It was round about this time in my life journey that I started to take notice of girls. There was one girl who laid siege to my teenage mind for a short period during my second year of secondary schooling. Her name was Jean Thompson. She was a year below me in Bella, and though I had seen her around, in school corridors and in the swing-park, we'd never exchanged words. The 'Swingies', as the park was known, form an important element in my story. A popular meeting place among the youth of Ibrox/ Govan, the swing-park was bounded on four sides by the blocks of the slum clearance housing scheme which stood next to our red sandstone tenement. The streets which bordered the swing-park, distinguished by its 'American' swings, were Brand Street, Whitefield Road, Ibrox Street and Midlock Street. These swings were strange, exotic structures. They were nothing like the sissy, single seat on chains affairs you can see in television adverts nowadays when some mèirleach, thief is trying to get you to buy something by showing an adult, a parent perhaps, bonding with a toddler by pushing the child ever and ever higher. American swings consisted of long slabs of thick wood that you straddled, gripping tightly one of six iron hoops embedded at intervals in the wood. The entire length of the wood was suspended from four long columns of tubular steel supported on either side by a steel skeletal frame that resembled nothing more than outline of a house roof before the tiles went on. The deal was that a pair of lads would stand upright at either end of the slab and, gripping a pair of columns each, would use one foot to propel the passengers or single passenger backwards and forwards on the wooden slab at dizzying speed.

I'd noticed Jean and her older sister Sandra a few times at this venue, but all I knew about them was that they lived in a ground level flat at the top end of Whitefield Road. I didn't speak to her until one Saturday afternoon we found ourselves together in a queue waiting to get into a matinee showing of some film or other. (If you had a shilling to spare on a Saturday afternoon you willingly spent a tanner (sixpence) at the turnstile of the Capital Picture House at Lorne School to see The Jolson Story or …anything really, and if you had the coupons, you blew the other tanner on a bar of milk toffee and a sherbet dab in Stark's Sweet Shop next to Bobby Crawford's newspaper shop in Ibrox Street.) It might have been Big Iain MacGibbon who accompanied me that afternoon, but the events that followed my formal introduction to Jean Thompson and her sister Sandra wiped clean every peripheral memory of that day, and I can't remember if it was Gus Matheson or somebody else who was my picture-going companion. I felt the tap on my shoulder.

"What? Me?" I point at myself.

"No, Willie Waddle of Rangers," a blond girl, slightly taller than me, says.

I don't know how to reply to this sarcastic girl. I look closely at her, from the bottom up. The feet in black sneakers, tanned bare legs up to a mid-thigh tartan skirt, a small waist and the sharp bulge of her breasts confined by the familiar blue and gold sweatshirt of our school.

144

"You Norrie Maclean?"

"Ah, yes."

"Got a girlfriend?"

"Absolutely, yeah …no, actually."

This girl doesn't waste time. She's quite …attractive, really. Her eyes are dark and her mouth is wide and open and I glimpse lots of white teeth as she smiles down at me – she's definitely smiling. I wonder how I didn't notice how pretty – apart from the height – she was when I saw her in school or at the 'American' swings.

"Jean," she says, swivelling towards her even taller pal, "and this is my sister Sandra." She leans towards me. "Do you mind if we sit beside you when we get inside?"

I think about what a real alpha male would say, and it occurs to me that I may in fact be like, you know, a theta male. I try to keep my voice deep and level: "That'd be great, Jean."

"Do you think I'm good-looking, Norman?"

"Yeah," I gulp. I'm losing even my theta maleness.

"What's it like to be the heart-throb of the second year?"

"Hey, Jean, don't take advantage of Norrie," her sister says. Sandra is a senior in fourth year and is reputed to have a boyfriend who is a cadet policeman.

Jean addresses her sister: "Shut up, Sandra. He's a cute bit o' stuff."

"He's not a 'bit of stuff', you're just out to embarrass him."

"This is pure garbage!" Jean stamps her feet on the spot. "You don't like me to have any fun, Sandra. I think you're just jealous about all the boys who fancy me rotten."

"Come on, Jean, enough."

Jean tucks her arm in mine, laughs and whispers. "I'll be your girlfriend if you want, Norrie."

For the ten minutes or so, after we are admitted to the cinema, my experience is like an out-of-body one. The seating arrangements that Jean has skilfully directed have me in an aisle seat at the far end of a row, Jean seated to my right, Sandra beyond her. We settle in to follow the ritual of 'going to the pictures'. First of all you viewed the 'adverts', then the 'trailers', titillating excerpts for coming attractions, the 'wee' film and, finally, the 'big' picture or main feature. It is at the conclusion of the advertisements, an element everybody ignores, that Jean whispers to me. The screen is filled with the corporate logo of the company who produced the handful of clips that have gone before. A giant orange circle encloses the white letters TP in block capitals.

"Know what these letters stand for?"

"Don't know. Don't really care."

"Are ye ready for this? They stand for Thompson Prostitutes!" Jean hisses.

Oo-er, she might only be a wee – well, not so wee – first year, but she is coming out the shop when I am only going in. She is displaying an alarmingly familiarity with … 'it'.

"I hear you're pretty good at French, Norrie. Is that right?"

All I can do is catch my breath and squint sideways for signs. Jean slithers forward.

"You want to help me with my French?"

"Yeah," I gulp.

"Good," she says, and there's heat on my knee and a hand moving up my leg. She leans in. "Next Tuesday after tea in the swing-park." The hand encloses my thigh. "Mah sister's got a date then, and I'll have the whole house to myself."

"Don't you dare take that boy back to ours, Jean!" Sandra, who has been listening, says.

"Shut up, you old boot!" Jean shouts and kicks her sister.

"Ow!"

Without warning, Sandra rises to her full five foot ten and sqeezes past the pair of us and walks quickly up to the exits.

I look behind me for her: gone.

"Look, forget her," Jean says. "She's no good for you. See you on Tuesday." She stands up – must be at least five nine – and as I look up at her she flicks her tongue round her lips and takes my hands and puts them on the front of her school top and lets me feel what I now know I've wanted for months. She walks slowly away from me up the aisle. At the swing doors she turns and gives me a wink.

Whit happened, Norrie?" It's Big Iain MacGibbon. He's three seats down and leaning sideways. "Whit's going ona wi' these lassies?"

"Nothing," I say. "Everything's *ala keefik*." I'm not sure, but I think this is Arabic slang for 'everything's fine'. We learned this kind of patter from older young men who had served in Egypt during National Service.

"Dae ye want tae go oot efter them?"

"No, sit back and enjoy the picture, Iain."

What picture or film am I referring to? I'll never know. I am too busy constructing fantasies of my own to pay much attention to the imaginings of some American film director. Everything is indeed very fine. Is this fluttering in the tummy an index of delights to come? Is this a promise that my busy little life will soon be invaded by ...like ...you know ...well, *love*?

Of course, even at a young age, I knew that 'love' always carries the risk that one may be rejected. There was a certain Tuesday night in the summer of 1952 in the 'swingies'. I am seated midway along the wooden carriageway of one of the 'American' swings with a brown paper bag containing the *Nouveau Cours de Français* on an adjacent seat my highly brogue shoes swinging idly backwards and forwards inches above the ground. I am the most fragrant male in all of SW1. Copious splashes of aftershave have ensured that. My grooming seems to have little effect on Jean Thompson who has both hands clamped on the bar, the one that looks like the ridge pole of a house, that lies parallel to and about eight feet above the ground. She is dressed differently tonight –white 'sannies' red ankle socks, short black skirt and predominately blue checked short-sleeved blouse. She is hanging limply, almost motionless, and has been for at least four minutes, with her feet pointing down and no trace of exertion on her smiling face.. Maybe this is why she's so tall for her age. Now, I am pretty sensitive about how short I am compared to other boys in my year. To be looked down upon by a girl – a girl fully a year younger than me – is intolerable. I promise I'll return here when it gets dark, or even before I start my milk run tomorrow, and practise the hanging limp thing.

"Norman?" she says clearly without the hint of a tremor in her voice.

"Yes?" I reply guiltily. I'd rather jump from the Finnieston crane than disclose my future training programme to her.

"Say something in French."

I concentrate. "*C'est impossible dit le vent. Elle est dans la rivière* …"

"No, scrub that. Can you sing?"

"I …" Unable to think up a lying answer quickly enough, I stammer: "I only know Gaelic songs. We talk Gaelic at home." Wait a minute: what about that folk song that drunk guy from Paisley sang at the Lorne Street Ceilidh a fortnight ago?

I've made a song just for you, Jean." I smile.

"What's it called?"

"It's called …er, I Love My Jean."

Jean traverses the bar, hand over hand, until she is able to place both her feet on the supporting strut, an iron pole that extends to the ground at an angle of forty-five degrees. She leans back and her blond hair falls away from her face and she smiles down at me. "Right, my wee Hector friend, off ye go."

"Okay." I get up and begin the recital, attempting to duplicate the thick Ferguslie accent of the drunk I heard singing it first.

'Ah love mah Jean,
Ma bonnie, bonnie Jean,
She's verra temperamental,
And she's only seventeen.

It's a very bad voice, like a rook cawing. My tongue is thickening. I'm rushing the words out. I'm speeding through them as if in embarrassment or sorrow at how naff the lyrics are. These words keep bunching in my teeth.

"Mmmmmm," Jean murmurs, putting her thighs on either side of the slanty pole. With a jerk of her upper body she transfers her double handed grip from the horizontal bar to the top of the support pole above her head. The entire length of her body, neck, breasts, belly, thighs and crossed calves, is now entirely draped over the metal support. She grins like the big conspirator that she is, and slowly, slowly, ever so slowly she edges downwards.

I magically find my voice and disregarding the kitsch lyrics sing like Benjamino Gigli in the La Scala.

Her hair is awfu' curly,
And her cheek is like the rose,
And she comes frae Bonnie Scotland
Where the bluebell grows.

By the time I get to the last line, Jean has alighted, stepped round the base of the pole and holds out her hands to me. I take them with both of mine and give the number the big finish. She has big hands: maybe my hands are kind of small. I've knocked out Malky with these hands of mine.

"Ha," she gasps. "Come on, Norrie. Back tae mine." Gosh, this girl doesn't hang about. She now has both her big hands round my waist and she tugs me towards her. Jean Thompson, though chronologically younger, is an experienced older woman. This feels so good. Forget everything, a *Thormoid*. Go with her.

UNE LIAISON DANGEREUSE

"Where's your sister?" I ask, my hands still enclosed in hers as I draw back.

"I told you," Jean snaps. "She's on a date with her boyfriend, him that's a police cadet. He takes her to the pictures up the toon." As she speaks, she releases one hand, and with the other tugs me in her wake as she makes for the Whitefield Road exit.

We stumble into the Thompson flat, first right low-down as you enter the close. We have the place to ourselves right enough. In the kitchen we stand facing each other, our faces no more than ten inches apart.

"Do you want to do the French thing?" She tilts her head.

"Oh, no!" I slap my forehead at my stupidity. "I've left the French grammar book in the swing park."

"Forget it, Norrie," she giggles. Her hand twitches around mine. "You have to learn to relax. You're not like all these other boys who're only after the one thing. You're really … I don't know …innocent."

"Huh," I'm not sure what to say.

"Huh … ehm … well …" I'm stuttering.

"Do you want to see our bedroom?"

This is maybe a bad idea. It's a bad idea as much as it's a bad idea to walk up to Mulrine and to punch him on the nose, but I've now lost all hope. She leads me to the room she shares with her big sister.

She's standing right in front of me. Her curved glossy lips are slightly parted and her sparkling dark eyes are looking down at my forehead. Suddenly she leans forward and grabs my shoulders. She pushes me back on to one of the twin beds that furnish the room. With surprising ease she flips me over so that my thin body covers her more substantial one. She has both her hands clamped to the back of my head by this time and her long fingers are energetically ruffling my hair which is slightly damp with sweat.

"Do you want to do it, Norrie?" she asks.

I nod, and pull away with my eyes tight shut. I look up at her chin. My legs are sticking out from the end of the bed.

"Shagging!" I hear from the doorway.

It's the sister.

"Shagging on my bed. You're nothing but a dirty slut, Jean!" She runs over to us and drags me off and, holding me close to her ample front, carries me to the doorway. She deposits me there and turns to her sister on the bed.

"I told you not to harass this wee boy, Jean," she says shaking her finger. "And I catch you making love on my bed."

"Hey, wrinkly," Jean retaliates. "It wasn't just me, right? Norrie was on top of me. And we didn't have sex."

"You would have let him, if Douglas hadn't been asked to do an extra shift tonight and I hadn't come home and caught you at it."

"Sandra, away and bile yer can! And you can blow too, Norrie!"

"Um, okay!" I answer into Sandra's back. I try to think of something suitable, witty even, to say to Jean. "Ah … j'ai eu le grand plaisir de faire ta connaissance, cherie … mais c'est domage que …"

"Aw, belt up!" Jean shouts from the bed.

"Yeah," Sandra says, gesturing towards the door behind her. "Don't mind if I don't see you out, son."

I stomp my way down the hallway, slamming the soles of my highly polished brogues against the linoleum. Once outside in Whitefield Road I think about the events of the evening as I walk slowly home. I cannot decide whether I've been lucky or unlucky, the way things turned out.

At the corner of Midlock Street and Brand Street a familiar figure is playing keepie-up with a tennis ball. Big Iain MacGibbon, *an gille aig Màiri Fhraochain a Loch a' Chàrnain,* the son of Mary daughter of *Fraochan from Loch Carnan,* is doing what all the boys do when there's nobody out playing in the street. He sees me approaching and stuffs the ball into a trouser pocket. He's still in short trousers, while I have recently acquired my first pair of 'longies'.

"Hi-ya, Norrie."

"Hi-ya."

"Where hiv ye been, Norrie?

"Tap o' Whitefield Road."

"Yer hair's like a burst fag."

"Ah know." I sweep a hand over the top of my head. "That wis yon bird done that." Syntax goes 'oot the windae' when you're adopting a pose of insouciance.

"That Jean wan?"

"Actually her big sister was in the bedroom as well."

"You were ben the room wi' two birds?"

"Ah … that's right."

"There wis three o' yous there, Norrie?"

I am silent for a few seconds. Then I decide to go for it. I look right into Big Iain's eyes and turn my palms upward in a what-can-you-do gesture. "Yeah," I say in tones of false humility, "I suppose you could say that."

"Geez, whit wis it like?"

"Garbage."

"Whit?"

"I'm telling you it was rubbish."

"How?"

"Urr ye ready furr this, Iain? They bullied me right there in the room wi' the twin beds!"

"Naw!"

"Aye, they were fighting. Ah think it wis o'er me. And they're both big girls."

"Right."

"Ah wisnae gonnae pit up wi' a cat fight wi' me jist staunin' there like a spare, know whit ah mean?"

"Right."

"So ah goat oot. Jist went right up the touchline."

"Wid ye go back there?"

"Never. They took advantage o'me, so they did. Is that no' terrible? I mean that's a pure liberty!"

"You mean they forced ye tae dae things."

"Didnae gi'e them the chance. Ye cannae trust girls who're bigger than you."

"Ah wid say so, Norrie."

"It's disgustin', that's whit it is, pal."

"Sounds like that pair hiv scunnert ye, Norrie."

"Ah widnae go as far as 'scunnered.' Really, ah'm no' sae sure. Sometimes ah think they've pit me aff women. Sometimes ah wonder if ah should gi'e lassies another chance."

"But no' wi' any burrd fae Whitefield Road, right?"

"Ah'll tell ye wan thing."

"Whit's that?"

"Whitefield Road's a thing of the past."

"Ye can say that again."

"Whitefield Road's a thing of the past."

We both laughed.

"Whit dae ye think aboot Rangers' chances next season?"

I stopped laughing.

Big Iain MacGibbon reached into his pocket and took out the tennis ball.

"Want tae play a game o''heidies', Norrie?"

"Okay."

We face each other with eighteen feet of pavement between us. MacGibbon tosses the ball up about three feet into the air, much in the same way that professional tennis players do on TV when serving. As the ball descends, he snaps his head back quickly and, wrenching his neck forward, smashes it fiercely with his temple towards me. The pace is fast, but the direction poor. I catch it easily and, following the same ritual, toss it up and head it to his far right. He whiffs the catch, and it's one up for me. He directs a cunning header towards my feet and the bounce deceives me. Goal to MacGibbon. And on we play.

JAMES, SON OF MURDOCH

It's 5.30pm on a Monday evening in late May. My sister Lorna and I are seated at the kitchen table in 191 Brand Street and looking open-mouthed at the exotic creature lounging in my father's 'Big' chair, back to the window and next to the fireplace. The object of our rapt attention is *Seumas Mhurchaidh*, James son of Murdoch, or, in English, James Macdonald of Griminish, Benbecula. I always get a palpable high in his company. For one thing, during all the time my mother and I stayed with him in Uist he always talked to me like I was a person, an intelligent youngster worthy of respect. My sister, eight years of age, isn't too familiar with James, and she focuses on his appearance. He is short, well, a lot shorter than my father, but I suspect he probably weighs about the same. His heavily muscled forearms rest on the wooden arms of the 'Big' chair. They are the colour of teak. He has rolled up the sleeves of his white dress shirt and discarded a black tie and detachable collar to reveal a weird contrast in his skin pigmentation. His veined forearms are deeply tanned up to a point just below his elbows. Above that, his skin is the colour of milk. A similar, almost striped effect is apparent in his face and neck. Above the line where his grandpa shirt cuts across his throat up to his receding hairline he is deeply tanned. Below the line his partially exposed chest is white. Lorna whispers to me out the corner of her mouth: "He's just like 'Boysie'." This is a reference to out ginger and white cat, and I shush her with a stern look and a raised finger to my lips. James doesn't seem to be offended by Lorna's interjection. Indeed, ever since I got to know him way back at the start of WW11 when my mother and I went to stay with him in Eilean Mòr, Griminish in Benbecula, Seumas Mhurchaidh has always behaved with all the circumspection of an uninhibited pirate. He exudes the air of easy authority that comes from persisting day after day in wresting a livelihood as a marginalised crofter from sour land in a hostile climate. His short but bulky legs are stretched out on the carpeted floor of the kitchen, crossed at the ankles. His thighs and calves bulge against the coarse serge of his Sunday suit. He's slumped low in my dad's chair and winking at me. Oxymoron or no, what James, son of Murdoch, son of Angus, son of Big John, looks like is a kind of genial, sawn-off giant.

The reason I like *Seumas Mhurchaidh* is that he's a real cool guy. An account of how he conned a *Barrach*, a native of Barra, who was selling whisky from the SS Politician door to door throughout Benbecula back in 1942 is simply too fraught with litigious potential to be tackled. No, I'm not going to do that.

The presence of *Seumas Mhurchaidh* in our home means that I am being farmed out, yet again, for a week to the larger flat of *Cailleach Tait*. The home of my granny's best friend is situated about half a mile away on Paisley Road West, but to me it may as well be in St Kilda as far as social intercourse is concerned. I don't know any of the young people who live in the posh end of Ibrox, but I'm not at all concerned about the lack of potential playmates in that patch because I'll be involved with my own wee gang playing 'Three and in' or 'Statues' or even 'Peever' in Midlock Street until it gets dark. Then, instead of heading round the corner to my home, I'll trot up to Ibrox Street, turn right towards Whitefield Road, cut right into Ibrox Oval, turn right onto Edminstone Drive, veer left at Merrick Gardens and turn sharp right on to Paisley Road West. This mini-migration is a move I am obliged to make, on at least three occasions each year, whenever someone from Uist needs a bed in my parents' house. I don't mind. The *cailleach* and her spinster daughter *Seasaidh* are good to me, and send me off to school each morning with a good hot breakfast inside me. The bachelor son, Dòmhnall, in his mid-fifties, is a driver on the Glasgow Underground railway, and I've never seen him out of the bottle green Corporation livery. He is also a piper and he frequently entertains *Dòmhnall Eàirdsidh* 'Star Cottage', Donald Archie Macdonald, and *Dòmhnall Mhurchaidh*, Donald MacMillan from Griminish, Benbecula in his dining room where they swap practice chanters and tunes. I was by no means reluctant to strut my stuff at these informal recitals and basked in the approval of these piping aficionados.

Of course, I only sleep and have breakfast in Cailleach Tait's house. Dinner (lunch) and what I persist in calling 'tea' is prepared by my mother, Peigi Bheag, and this is what she is doing over at the stove behind the 'Big' chair as Lorna and I wait for the stew and potatoes to be served. She pretends to be shocked by the invasion of her territory by her first cousin, and so does my wee sister too, at least externally. Lorna doesn't really know our guest and at eight years of age she always takes her cue from her mother. I, on the other hand, spent the happiest days of my boyhood under his roof and I am thrilled at the man's pose of insouciance.

The reason for James's presence in our home is that he is 'out' for the Annual General Assembly of the Church of Scotland, which takes place in May of every year in Edinburgh.

Though he is a fully accredited elder in the Church of Scotland, Griminish, Benbecula *Seumas* doesn't really 'do' the General Assembly. Other elders from far-flung parishes all find lodgings in the capital for the duration of the event, but James, because of familial piety or some other reason, prefers to spend the week with his cousin, *Peigi Bheag*, in Glasgow. Apart from a brief attendance at the obligatory convocation on the Saturday morning, he spends the following week in Glasgow. His MO for 'Assembly week' is as follows: after a high-cholesterol Kamikaze breakfast he sallies forth in full Sunday church-going garb – highly polished six-eyelet black boots, coarse navy blue serge suit, white shirt, black tie and homburg - and conducts a slow-paced and extremely leisurely *paseo* along the Paisley Road West, stopping frequently at 'Teuchter' watering holes along the way. At that time, over sixty years ago, in the south-west quadrant of Glasgow in an area embracing the districts of Tradeston, Kinning Park, Plantation, Ibrox and Govan, thousands of natives of North and South Uist, Eriskay and Barra have settled. If you had the price of a 'half and a half-pint' in your pocket it wasn't difficult to find congenial, Gaelic-speaking company in the many pubs, from Pollok Street to Govan Cross, that catered to this Island demographic.

I know this pattern of behaviour to be true and unvarying. I recall being assigned by my mother the previous year to follow James during his daylight peregrations. I had employed extremely sophisticated surveillance techniques – you know, whirling round suddenly to present my back to James when he stopped to admire some desirable object in a window display, popping round corners, darting in and out of tenement closes – so that I was able to report to my mother that the *Badhlach* seemed to be incapable of passing any 'Teuchter' pub between Kingston and Lorne School without spending at least a quarter of an hour inside.

What I didn't report to my mother at the evening de-briefing was that I had blown my cover and that *Seumas* had discovered I had been trailing him all afternoon. What happened was that I had been getting a wee bit bored with keeping a distant eye on the happy wanderer and I became somewhat careless, even a tad rash. After all, it didn't take the deductive powers of a Sherlock Holmes to ascertain where *Seumas* went on his daily jaunts. He went to 'Teuchter' pubs. That was his thing during General Assembly week. He didn't go to daffodil tea parties or to the local library to take part in book-reading clubs. He went to the Clachan, the Quaich, the Viceroy, the Kyles of Bute, the Stanley, Joe Fleck's and the Regano.at Paisley Road Toll. It was at the last of these public houses that I experienced a humiliation that, surprisingly, turned out quite well for me. I was standing on the north side of Paisley Road leaning nonchalantly against a lamp post just in front of the Imperial Picture House (now the Grand Old Opry) when I saw James surging across Admiral Street with the gait of the crofter – *ceum na mòintich*, the stride of the moorland – and suddenly veering to his right an entering the Lounge Bar of the Regano (now the Merchants' Quay). After scampering across the road I resolved to find out what went on inside these dark enclosures that gave off spicy fragrances. Fortunately there was a plate glass window to the left of the Lounge Bar entrance. Unfortunately the lower half of the pane was coated in black paint. Above this, about seven feet clear of the pavement, there was a band of transparent glass. If I could somehow hoist myself up so that my head would stick up beyond the tinted band, then the interior and the clientele of this mysterious place would be revealed. There was an extremely narrow and slanted window ledge situated about three feet up from the ground, and by standing on my tiptoes and placing enormous strain on my calf and thigh muscles I succeeded in getting the top of my head, my eyes and rather prominent nose above the lower black expanse of window.

Seumas Mhurchaidh, James son of Murdoch, was standing on the right hand arc of my vision with his back to the counter. With his stocky legs parted and his thumbs in his belt he radiated alpha-male bonhomie. Behind him the chargehand of the pub, wearing a white apron, was performing complicated sleight of hand movements with two pint glasses and metal spout on a foot high beer dispenser from which issued a steady trickle of dark liquid. This was Peter MacEachan from South Uist whom I recognised as a regular attendee at the Saturday night Uist and Barra ceilidhs in the Orange Halls in Lorne Street. James was grinning at a couple of *bodaich* seated opposite him on a tweed-covered bench fronted by a heavy wooden table. These old men were swaying from side to side, but judging by their vigorous hand clapping they seemed to be enjoying what I guessed to have been James's recent rendition of a song or a gout of *bàrdachd*, poetry. Mouth agape, he raised his chin to the ceiling in delighted appreciation of a witty remark made by either one of the old men or himself. In a millisecond he clocked me. Despite the fact that only my eyes and nose cleared the tinted section of the window, adding a Kilroyishly surreal aspect to my intrusion, James recognised me and with both arms extended and his hands flapping he invited me to join the company inside the Lounge. I promptly accepted his invitation, whereupon he ordered a glass of whisky for me. Peter and an old retired policeman from Fersit in Lochaber called Angus Campbell, in a tactful and loving way, suggested that perhaps a double measure of rotgut wasn't a suitable refreshment for a lad who was underage. In an only just discernible hand wave to the present day campaign of drinkaware, these wise men settled on a pint of 'Happy Day' for your correspondent. This concoction, no longer fashionable, consisted of a half pint of draught 'light' beer fortified by a 'wee dump' of bottled strong ale. As we bumped our way back along the Paisley Road West towards Brand Street and home, Seumas told me that he had spotted me right start of his afternoon excursion. "*Och, a ghraidhein,* Och, dear boy," he said, "*Is fhada bhon a mhothaich mi dhut a' cur nan caran mar*

160

Ottaman air truinnsear, I noticed you a long time ago spinning like an Ottoman on a plate." (I didn't understand his simile until much later. The spinning Ottaman referred to a Turkish dervish.) As Seumas repeatedly thrust his hip against mine, forcing me to stagger into the odd passerby, he talked about characters from Uist and what they were renowned for. They were identified by *sloighnidhean* or patronymics – you know, John son of Roderick son of Farquhar or Joan daughter of Malcolm son of Joseph – and very quickly my head turned into porridge trying to identify the protagonists of his many anecdotes. I resolved to ask him about my own maternal forebears in Uist sometime in the future at a time when my brain might be less clouded.

MURCHADH BEAG SIONSAIN

Another year passes and *Seumas Mhurchaidh 'ic Aonghais 'ic Iain Mhòir* has invaded our family again. He's slumped in my father's chair and my mother is standing behind him at the cooker and looking a little narrow-eyed at his large right hand as it slithers down the outside arm of the chair towards a half-full bottle of whisky on the hearth where he has placed it earlier for easy-grope retrieval.

"An gabh mi òran dhuibh, Will I give you a song?" he enquires as he brings the uncorked neck of the bottle up to his lips.

"Cha ghabh, No," *Peigi Bheag* barks.

James ignores her, takes a swig from the bottle and starts to howl. In an awesomely out of tune voice, at full volume, he attacks a Gaelic love song.

"An cluinn thu mi, mo nighean donn, Can you hear me, my brown-haired maid?"

Dèan èist is thoir an aire dhomh, Listen and pay attention to me:

Tha mòran dhaoin' sa bharail seo, Many people are of this opinion,

Gur òg an leannan dhomh-s' thu, That you were only young when you became my beloved.

"An ann an Hiort a tha do leannan, Is it in St Kilda your sweetheart is?" says my mother in a thinly veiled reference to the volume employed by her cousin.

"A Sheumais?" I interject in an attempt to avoid things escalating into a full-scale rammy.

"Seadh, What?"

"Bheil sibh math air sloinneadh, Are you any good at genealogy?" I ask.

Meadhanach math air na daoine a bhuineas dhomh fhìn, Fairly strong on the people in my own family."

"Who was the Murdoch in your own patronymic?" I asked him in English, in deference to my sister's poor grasp of Gaelic.

"Your grannie's young brother."

"Right." I said. "He was *Murchadh mac Aonghais 'ic Iain Mhòir* Murdoch, son of Angus, son of Big John."

"Aye, that was on his paternal side."

I sense that Lorna is more than a little bored with our dialogue. Her harrumphs through clenched teeth are becoming increasingly audible. I'm unable to let go.

"Who was his mother, then?"

"Caitriona Mhòr, nighean Mhurchaidh Bhig, Big Kate, daughter of Little Murdoch."

"So your father was called after his maternal grandfather?"

"Correct."

"And who was Little Murdoch and what's his back story?"

James cocks his head to one side and puts on a cold smile. *"Murchadh Beag Sionsain,* Little Murdoch Johnson, lived most of life in *Baile nan Cailleach,* Nunton, Benbecula," he says as he sinks back into my father's big chair. "But for a while when he was aged about fourteen it looked as if he'd leave Uist for good and never see the island again."

"How?"

"He was taken with his two brothers, Angus and Alasdair, from their home on Nunton Moor by land officers in the employ of the estate owner. These agents of the evictions hog-tied the wrists of the two older lads behind their backs with coarse hempen ropes, and then they hog-tied their ankles in the same way, and then they ran a length of rope from their wrists to their ankles."

"Little Murdoch too?"

"No, he was not fully-grown and the bailiffs just tied his wrists together, in front of him, before they threw all three young men into a cart. They were to be transported to an emigrant ship moored off Lochboisdale."

When said the words "emigrant ship", Seumas Mhurchaidh sat upright and slid forward to the edge of the chair and exclaimed: "*Clann an Fhir nach can mi*, Spawn of the one I won't mention!"

"You're kidding!"

"That's what I said myself when my grandmother, *Caitrìona Mhòr nighean Mhurchaidh Bhig*, Big Kate daughter of Murdoch Johnson, told me about the abduction of her father and uncles. I said at the time: '*Tha sibh a' tarraing asam*, You're making fun of me.' She wasn't."

My uncle James – I know, he's my mother's first cousin, but I call him uncle James – rises to his feet. "I am going to tell you the story of Little Murdoch," he says with the faintest of smiles." Go, James, go!

"In 1838," he intones in his best General Assembly voice, "Clanranald, now a dapper young regency buck in the society circles of London, was in deep financial trouble. Fast living in London –cotillions graced by pretty, high born ladies, drinking claret in exclusive gentlemen's clubs – came at a price. One of the money lenders to whom he owed money caught up with the young Clanranald in Vauxhall one evening. He says, 'Scuse me, young sir. You've got estates in Scotland, I've got the power of the

Law on my side. I want some money."'

"What happened then?"

Uncle James starts pacing backwards and forwards in front of the fireplace. He rubs his hands together.

"Oh, Clanranald said that the Benbecula estate wasn't worth a great deal. The money-lender said, 'Sell it!' The young chieftain admitted that his South Estate might be worth a bit more. The money lender said, 'Sell it!' and eventually he was forced to sell his estates in Benbecula, South Uist and Barra to Colonel John Gordon of Cluny, probably the most hated man in Scotland in the mid-nineteenth century. To this monster, who referred to the inhabitants of the southern Hebrides as 'aborigines', the preferred method of raising income had an elegant simplicity. Populations oppressed by dislocation, removal, congestion and poverty now the kelp boom was over were simply superfluous. The way forward, obviously, was to get rid of these small tenants and landless cottars and convert the land into large sheep farms. Enforced emigration to America provided the means to this end."

I see Lorna arching her eyebrows and spreading her eyes wide.

"So, that's why the Johnson brothers were evicted?" I ask incredulously.

"Now, while it is certainly true," *Seumas* continued, "that there was measurably less congestion and poverty in Benbecula than in South Uist and Barra this would have offered little comfort to the brothers Johnson who were living with their widowed mother on the moor of Benbecula in a windowless bothy when the factor and a posse of ground officers lifted them from their dwelling. The emigrant ship, already packed with dispossessed folk from Tiree, Barra, Eriskay and South Uist was their destination".

The way *Seumas Mhurchaidh* tells it, up in Lochboisdale, South Uist, while Murdoch's two older brothers, young men in their physical prime, were being manhandled aboard an open tender, the slight young boy, small even for his fourteen years, wriggled free. There was only one thing left to do! Nothing else left! He swung his leg over the side of the cart and got a toe-hold on the rim of the wheel. Then he swung the other leg over and dropped to the ground. One of the ground officers yelled out, 'Hey! Stop him! STOP HIM!' Murdoch made a dash for *Beinn Ruigh Choinnich* at full speed. Pursued by ground officers and baying mastiffs with drooling, snapping teeth he raced to the summit. The scree on the mountainside was so hard on his bare feet he could fell blood slipping beneath his soles.

Seumas stands still and starts to make swimming motions with both his arms, opening and snapping shut his fingers in imitation of someone grasping at clumps of heather and hauling himself upward. My mother serves the stew and leaves the room. Lorna and I ignore the steaming plates. We can't take our eyes off James.

"The boy in time lost his pursuers." James continues. "All except one. A huge giant of a man in a rust coloured Inverness cape and and a floppy Balmoral bonnet on his head was closing in on him. The man's right hand held a long metal sword and his left fist is clenched a leather leash attached to the collar of a salivating mastiff."

James pauses and scans his audience for what would be some rhetorical effect. His last words bring a gasp and a whinny from my sister who is suddenly thrilled by the prospect of imminent violence.

"The dog was released and it leaped upon the chest of Murdoch. The boy was sprawled on his back, his hands stretched out to the sides. The helpless boy resorted to gabbled prayer.

> *Tha rud is feàrr na chòir a seo*
> *Tha dòrn an t-sagairt mhòir a seo*
> *Tha rud is feàrr na chairbh a seo*
> *Tha ceann an duine mhairbh a seo ...*

A thing better than right is here,
The fist of the big priest is here,
A thing better than the carcase is here,
The head of the dead man is here ...

"His body was drenched with sweat. Very soon, his face and chest were drenched with the dog's blood, because the giant had cut the animal's throat. 'Run! Now!' the giant bellowed. Murdoch was confounded. He sprang to his feet spun about and ran towards the summit."

Lorna has twisted her lips into a half smile. I begin to move my head lowly from side to side.

"The way I see it," uncle James says, leaning towards his audience, his eyes blazing, "it's high time that more of our young men should show similar spirit."

Is he hinting that I am lacking in courage? Is he singling me out? Is he just letting his eyes linger on me longer than Lorna?

"Did he make it home safely?" This from Lorna whose eyes are as big as saucers.

"Over a period of six weeks he traversed the spine of South Uist, climbing and descending *Triuirebheinn, Stùlabhal, Beinn Mhòr* and *Beinn Choradail* and swimming the narrows of *Loch Aineort* and *Loch Sgiopoirt*. all the while pressing northward to Benbecula. He relied on the kindness of abandoned women folk in *bruchlaigean thaighean*, wretched, tumbledown huts, and often slept, cold and damp, in caves and among rocks." I am dumbfounded. I fight back the impulse to say "You're kidding."

"Obviously the kid made it home to *Sliabh na h-Airde* and was eventually allotted a croft in Nunton. He married Red-haired Catherine MacPherson, a Catholic lady from Liniclate, one of whose descendants, Colin MacPherson, became Bishop of Argyll and the Isles."

"And that was the story of your great-grandfather?" I ventured to say in a quivery voice. This stuff vibrates in my bones and resonates in my solar plexus and makes me feel that, yes, my ancestor did have a spirit that a hostile world outside could never exterminate.

"Just you two remember this," James, son of Murdo, launches into a peroration. "If *Murchadh Beag Sionsain*, Little Murdoch Johnson, hadn't escaped from Gordon of Cluny's ground officers, you children wouldn't be sitting here all cosy and snug and letting your tea grow cold. *Cha bhiodh sibh ann*, You wouldn't exist!"

Some time ago I received that email from a cousin of mine, Catriona Hamilton (née Johnson), a native of Benbecula now resident in Australia. She writes:

> '*I am sending you the research our American cousin George F Sanborn, now retired to Canada, has been doing on Prince Edward Island. Its in several parts and he apologized for it still being a draft copy. He has done an enormous amount of research over the past decades on the Uist people who went to North America. He was especially fascinated by the Johnsons because his Grand Mother was one of us!*'

Now, one of the legacies of my recovery from addiction has been a restored belief in the importance of truth. I clicked on George's link and discovered the following entry for my great-great grandfather:

> '*MURDOCH JOHNSON [Murchadh MacIain] (John[Iain]) was born at Uachdar, Benbecula, Parish of South Uist, Inverness-shire, Scotland, c1813-1816, and died. He married, probably in Benbecula, c1841, CATHERINE MacPHERSON [Catrìona Nic a' Phearsain*

*(NicMhuirrich)]. She was born at Balivanich, Benbecula,
c1814-1817, a daughter of Angus and Ann (MacPherson)
MacPherson [Aonghas and Anna (Nic a' Phearsain
[NicMhuirrich]) Mac a' Phearsain (MacMhuirrich)],
and died. Murdoch was a crofter and moved into the home
of his wife's parents at 19 Balivanich after his marriage
where they looked after his wife's widowed mother and
eventually became the tenants of the old MacPherson croft.
It contained 12 acres, 8 of which were arable, according
to the 1871 census. Census records consistently state that
Murdoch was born at Uachdar, Benbecula, which is in
accord with known facts of the family.'*

A pretty watery dram, don't you think? This is a history with no
potholes in it. There's no mention of him and his two brothers
being transported in chains to the emigrant ship moored off
Lochboisdale. We don't hear a bìg or a bèic about Murdoch's
escape from the ground officers and how an attacking savage
mastiff had its throat cut by one of the bailiffs.

Reading this account from across the Atlantic, based I'm sure
on credible research, I get a cold sweat on the back of my neck and
I think, 'Daingeadaidh! I've made a kind of a boo-boo here.' The
contrast between the vanilla blandness of the historical account
and Seumas Mhurchaidh's action-packed adventure story, not
to mention the liberties I myself took when writing a screenplay
based on the story brings the roses to my cheeks. My initial
response to the new information was to remain shtoom about the
entire thing and let the – how to put it? – fanciful versions stand
for all time, or at least for as long as I remain on this side of the
grass. Having pulled out most of my hair, I had already started
to tear at my eyebrows when I finally decided to recant in print.
Sure, James Macdonald of Griminish had a lot of the entertainer
in him. He didn't outright falsify things – he maintained he got

the story from his paternal grandmother, *Anna Mhòr* daughter of *Murchadh Beag Sionsain* – but sometimes the urge to flesh out the details and add to the suspense seemed to get the better of him. The common, pedestrian account of Murchadh Beag Sionsain's life may be the way it was in 1831, but I think that's a pretty boring way. I prefer stories to be a little bumpier. So did Seumas Mhurchaidh. The flights of fancy indulged in by Seumas and me appeal to my predilection for more colourful stories, but I concede that there were times when we were both guilty of going dangerously off-piste.

ME, THE CLASSICAL SCHOLAR

For me, a love of Latin as a kind of dim schoolboy at Bellahouston Academy in Glasgow in 1951 led me to Mone's Bar at the corner of the Govan Road and Carmichael Street where for two shillings and sixpence you, or one of your older-looking mates, could buy a half bottle of fortified British sherry bearing the legend 'Rich Ambrosia: Nectar of the Gods.' Eventually my affection for Bacchus, or Dionysus as he was known to Greek worshipers, transformed me into a fully-fledged member of the cult of Eleutharios, the Liberator, whose wine, music and ecstatic dance freed his followers from self-conscious fear. I was up for a ration of that. *Creid e a chlann*, Believe it, children. What I didn't believe, or didn't consider, in my early teens was that my devotion to the garish label on the flask which displayed a blousy Bacchus, his countenance an odd shade of burgundy, enveloped in large bunches of plump grapes coloured in hideous day-glo purple, would lay the foundation for a life-long whisky habit which was only broken in April 2010.

Allow me, please, to describe my moment of nostalgia, laced with masochism certainly, which took place on a wet, cold evening in November when I was fourteen years of age. When

Ross my pal told me what this drug was called – Rich Ambrosia - and where it could be purchased I had to sample it instanter. My two pals, Big Donald Macritchie and Ross MacMillan conducted our shared experiment in a back close in the Govan Road. As 'Tenement Teuchters' we were determined not to lead the kind of lives endured by our parents - merchant seamen and psychiatric nurse – and we all had Saturday jobs, paper and milk rounds. We had clubbed together to buy the vaunted elixir, and made the purchase price without difficulty. Yes, it was scary, dangerous, foolish thing we did, but no more so than lots of pranks we got up to back in the fifties. We smoked cinammon sticks, single Pasha cigarettes and went in for a lot of forbidden pursuits like listening to Radio Luxemburg on Sunday evenings and, when we could get away with it, engaging teenage girls in risqué banter and, very occasionally, indulging in sloppy kissing and sometimes even exchanging caresses of negligible puissance, but with what success is immaterial here. We were growing up into becoming greasy little *snàigearan* who practised flashy little backsteps in front of mirrored wardrobes in preparation for attendances at dances in the Highlanders' Institute and Govan Town Hall. We hoped to twinkle as little stars in the Highland Schottische and maybe to blow smoke into the bodices of love-starved girls bored with the attentions of geeks. In short, we generally qualified as libertines

We considered ourselves abandonnés of the first rank and we nominated Big Donald as the guy who just might pass as an eighteen year old to enter the 'snug' or Family Department of Mone's Bar to make the purchase. Ross and I stood outside feigning nonchalance for the seeming eternity the big fellow remained inside. At the point when MacMillan and I were debating the prudence of hanging around much longer, when it seemed clear that our intrepid leader had been rumbled and that he was, even as we spoke, divulging our names, addresses and collar sizes by means of the pub telephone to a desk sergeant in Orkney Street Police Station, the swing doors parted and Donald emerged grinning triumphantly. He tapped the inside pocket of his jacket confidently before giving us the thumbs up sign. In the parlance of addicts everywhere, we had scored.

We repaired in some haste to a close near St Columba's Copland Road Church. The minister of this Church of Scotland place of worship which conducted Gaelic services on Sundays was the Rev. 'Tommy' Murchison on whose congregation I had a brief, precarious toehold as a member of his Sunday School. I am sure that the Rev. Murchison would have found his clinical interest stimulated by the sequence of events in a spot within spitting distance of his place of work, if he hadn't been at home in Cardonald on that wet and windy mid-week evening. We, the musketeers, were huddled in the black close of the nearest tenement to the church at the time when Big Donald with a theatrical flourish wrenched the cork stopper from the bottle ... Talk about your turning points! The aroma of ethyl alcohol and, I swear, Woodbine cigarettes was pungent, and for those whose favourite tipple might have been creosote there could have been no greater thrill. Ever the gentleman, or the flyman, Big Donald proffered the flask to Ross, son of Hector MacMillan, Tiree, and Katie Ross, Skye. Employing the extravagant hand gesture of a Mafia Don, he indicated that the recipient should drink his fill. The recipient didn't. Handling the half bottle as though it were a small nuclear device, Ross, the most prudent member of our trio, through pursed lips, took a spinsterish sip of the vile infusion and with much gurning and spluttering expressed himself totally satisfied with his miniscule sample. Big Donald, son of Calum MacRitchie, Cross Skigersta Ness and Rachel Matheson, Baleshare, North Uist, grabbed the Rich Ambrosia impatiently and glug-glugged a good five ounces of the odious stuff before passing the wretched container on to yours truly. I knew from

173

the vivid puce of his countenance and the fetching drool of saliva issuing from Donald's open mouth that this was powerful gear. I was confident however that I possessed a potent trick up my sleeve, or, more accurately, in my blazer pocket, which would render my companions speechless with awe and guarantee my place in the pantheon of Teuchter or Hector folk heroes in Glasgow for all time.

I intended to do a Seumas Mòr. This was a long-contemplated stroke I had mentally rehearsed dozens of times since the idea of joining the Dionysian cult was first bruited. When I was much younger I had observed my maternal granduncle, James Macdonald of Old Mill, Griminish, Benbecula performing a peculiar ritual when downing a tot of whisky or rum from stubby little shot glasses. First of all, he'd cradle the base of the glass in the palm of one palm, ensuring its upright position by delicately spreading all five fingers round the sides. He'd offer a loud toast to the assembled company, lower his open mouth until his lips completely enveloped the rim, and then, with the glass firmly gripped between his teeth, he'd toss his head backwards and allow the spirit to flow from the upended receptacle down into his gullet. He'd then spit the container into the stone hearth where it would shatter into small pieces and finally he'd display his teeth in exultant triumph. Was this cool or what was it? Needless to say, this kind of theatrical performance appealed to my histrionic soul and I determined to replicate it with the fermented juice of the grape which I now held in my right hand.

The boys were suitably impressed when I extracted from the breast pocket of my school blazer a two-inch high shot glass I had borrowed from my mother's kitchen press. I mention en passant, or as we say in Gaelic, *dìreach mar fhacal*, this pocket above my rapidly beating heart was embroidered with an escutcheon enclosing the image of the eternal flame of knowledge supported by the Latin motto *Alere Flammam*. Ironies abound. With tremulous hand I filled the shot glass to the brim, all the time observing the niceties of the ceremony with digital dexterity. As I held the libation to my chin I intoned the toast gravely: *"Slàinte mhath is saoghal fada,* Good health and long life" before lowering my mouth towards the rim of the glass. It was odd I should wish for long life when I was on the point of losing mine.

The acrid liquid scorched tongue and throat lining. My lungs seriously underestimated the lethal power of the Nectar of the Gods and for all of three or four seconds refused to function. They tell me my five foot three inch frame folded gracefully into the foetal position on the grimy floor of the back close, and if Ross hadn't had the presence of mind to dig his fingers into my mouth to remove the shot glass, well, I should not have been able to go out on my milk run at six o'clock the next morning. Indeed, the verdict among the milk boys would have been, "Norrie's slept in again." "Aye," another would add, "I heard it was for good this time."

MacMillan's quick thinking saved the day ... and my life. Just as I was gagging horribly I heard Ross's solicitous whisper:

"Are you all right, Norrie?"

"Onnghh, onnghh, onnghh," I wheezed.

"I think he's developed a cleft palate," Big Donald mused, rather cruelly I thought.

I was hoisted upright by the helpful arms of my friends and frog-marched round the block a couple of dozen times until I recovered my breathing and my wits. Well, not my wits. I never did fully recover them. Oxygen deprivation undoubtedly damaged my cognitive ability for, despite my near-death experience with the Rich Ambrosia, with flushed face and weeping eyes I became a devotee of the ancient god *Bacchus*. And my adherence to the cult endured for almost sixty years.

BIG HEIST AT HAWKHEAD

"I've agreed a price with that van-boy in Galloway's the Grocers," my big pal Donald MacRitchie says.

"What kind of price?" I ask through pursed lips.

"Twenty pounds."

"Yeah, serious money. Can you trust him?"

"With my life, Norrie."

"Look, when we're talking about this heist, I want you to call me 'Hawk'."

I've always fancied being referred to as 'The Hawk.' Seems appropriate for a master criminal.

"What are you going to call me?"

"Oh, you'll be known as Do- wait … you'll be known as 'The Dove'."

"You're going to be the hawk that swoops on high, and I'm to be a common or garden pigeon?" Big Donald squeals in indignation.

"Listen, Do-er, Dove," I improvise recklessly. "The dove of peace is a kind of go-between, right? He's like Hermes, known as Mercury to the Romans, and is the messenger of the gods and he goes about with the help of a winged helmet and winged sandals."

Will Big Donald buy this gobbledegook?

"You want me to wear sandals and a helmet?" Donald asks.

"Naw. Just wear football boots and your St Mirren football strip."

"And what will you be wearing, Hawk?"

"On the night of the heist, I'll be wearing my Aston Villa strip and studded football boots."

"You're doolally. False names and weird clothes. I'm getting the wind up about this whole heist caper."

Alarma roja! Alarma roja! Is the big man having second thoughts about my master plan? It's the autumn of 1953. The two of us, Big Donald MacRitchie and I are talking in the Aldwych Café in Paisley Road West over dishes of vanilla ice cream liberally doused in raspberry sauce. This delicacy is known as a 'McCallum' and while we love the taste of this pink goo, we preferred the effect of Rich Ambrosia: Nectar of the Gods. For a 'McCallum' you need sixpence in old money. For a half bottle of Rich Ambrosia you need five times that, a half crown, twelve pence in today's cash. Long story short: our tastes in refreshments have become more expensive. We're hurting for money.

"Well, back to the heist, Do …er, Mercury," I say out the side of my mouth, taking an aggrieved look round the crowded café.

"What about it?"

"Look, I've thought it all through and I definitely want to do this."

"You look …er, Hawk," Donald says. "I've been thinking about this and I'm beginning to think I'm taking all the risks here."

"What risks?"

"This theft is happening on my patch, man. My father and mother both work in the Asylum. Even my mother's niece, Katie Mary, has started work in the Pavilion Ward. If anybody misses the gear, it won't take them long to figure out I'm responsible."

"It'll never happen, Mercury. I'm the guy who found the copper and I say our cut isn't big enough."

"What? A score isn't enough?"

"Not nearly. I want you, as a winged messenger, to go back to the van guy – John is it? - in Lambhill Street and tell him The Hawk wants more money."

"He'll not budge. Twenty's his limit."

Rubbish! I was down at the rag store in Broomloan Lane yesterday – you know, just round the corner from the Plaza Picture House on the Govan Road?"

"And?"

"And I asked the old man down there who's in charge of the store what he'd give us for a copper boiler, seven feet tall, and with a circumference of over eight feet."

"And?"

"He said it's worth a ton."

"A hundred pounds?"

"Tell your pal in Galloway's the Grocers that The Hawk's asking for fifty."

"I'll see what he says." Donald rises and heads westward.

I sit for a few minutes over a Senior Service cigarette. Maybe what I ought to feel now is dread. But it is a strange excitement that has dawned on me. There is planning involved in this little theft and I like that. I respond to that. I have a good feeling about the heist.

What we intend to steal is a big, really big, copper boiler that has been standing, abandoned obviously, for goodness knows how long, behind the Mortuary of Hawkhead Asylum – now Leverndale Hospital – in Crookston Road. (A little social history: In the fifties the lunatic asylum was the fiefdom of blood-pure Gaels, or, as they were known to Lowlanders, 'Hectors'. The Chief Superintendent was from Skye and all the Charge Nurses were from the islands. The reason for the over-representation of Hebrideans in this branch of health care was strength and physical stature. Compared to the native Glaswegians the 'Hectors' all enjoyed a healthy diet in their formative years. This physical superiority was important when disturbed poor souls suddenly experienced a manic outburst, and had to be subdued before they could harm themselves or others. Remember, this was at a time before the widespread and wholesale prescription of heavy tranquillizing drugs became popular. All these families with surnames like Macleod, Macneil, Macdonald, MacInnes, MacRitchie and Gunn lived in four-in-a-block houses owned by the hospital on Crookston Road. The sight of green rolling lawns and trees was heart pleasing to me, and I spent a lot of time in the grounds with Donald and his brother, Calum Angus, bird-nesting and generally mucking about. Our main passion was football and we practised dribbling, set pieces and diagonal passing on the soccer pitch in front of the administrative buildings. We hoped to get signed up by an amateur soccer outfit in nearby Paisley that was reputed to have ties to St Mirren FC.)

One day while rambling around the crumbling Mortuary building I notice a bulky tarpaulin-draped object standing seven foot high in front of a bricked up window. I whip the tarp off and a gleaming copper boiler is revealed. We quickly decide to steal it. Okay, I decided to steal it.

"Who'll buy it?" I muse aloud.

"I know a guy who drives a van for Galloway's, The Grocers in Lambhill Street, Kinning Park," says Donald.

"Do you think he'll act as a fence for us?"

"Certainly. He's well connected to 'Beef' Ramsay the moneylender from West Scotland Street. He knows Jim Macdonald from Plantation too."

"Get a price from him."

Three days later I get the price. This van guy is cheap. What if a truly talented guy, whose measurements correspond to my own, turned his considerable talents to the successful commission of a crime?

Surely loads of Glaswegians are at this very moment devoted to successful criminality and I just don't know about them because a large part of being a successful criminal means not getting caught. I think about all that as the cigarette smoke curls about my head but mostly I think about fifty pounds. I think about every single one of these pound notes, twenty-five quid each, on my way back home to Brand Street. At my current rate of earning it will take me the best part of eighteen months to earn twenty-five pounds. I'm going to be opening and closing those little umbrellas they give you for cocktails in the movies. Maybe the venue won't be in San Francisco but it could be in Saltcoats. Yeah, with that kind of dough I can buy 80 half bottles of Rich Ambrosia and another 80 packets of Woodbine cigarettes, and still have enough to impress Annag MacPherson or Archina MacIsaac or any of the Uist beauties I'm likely to meet at the dances in the Gym during the summer holidays. *Feumaidh mi m' fhoighidinn a ghlèidheadh.* All I have to do is exercise some patience.

On the following Saturday I'm standing on the touchline of the Hawkhead football pitch. Big Donald, in the black and white vertical stripes of St Mirren canters over to me.

"What did the van guy say, Mercury?"

"Forty…um, Hawk."

"Okay. We can live with that."

"Listen," Big Donald says with some urgency. "Let me save you some time OK?"

"What?"

"I'm not going to steal that boiler."

"You're not?"

"Correct. Because I don't want to try and steal it."

"You don't want your share of twenty pounds?"

"I do, but I don't want to go to jail or get a criminal record.

180

You know that when my time's out in the yards I want to become a police cadet, don't you?"

"Let me pose a hypothetical question, Mercury."

"What's a hypothetical question?"

"It's a question prefaced by a subordinate adverbial conditional clause – oh, forget it, man! Just answer this: If I guaranteed you success through proper planning, are you saying you still wouldn't do it?"

"I still wouldn't do it."

"Why not?"

"Because it would be wrong."

"Really? Are you giving me a moral objection, Mercury?"

"That's right."

"We're not in church any more, are we?' I say, my voice dripping sarcasm.

"Don't have to be in church to know right from wrong," Donald says in a mild tone of voice.

Neither of says anything after these exchanges.

I stewed over what I considered Big Donald's betrayal for about a week or so and then came to a conclusion. I walk to the twin telephone kiosks in Gower Street. One of them is operational: the other Donald and I have modified so that anybody placing their four pennies in the slot to pay for a call has their cash caught in a paper sling, meaning that pressing buttons A and B elicits no response. Later, using a kitchen knife, one of us punctures the sling. This releases the coins into the bowels of the apparatus. All we have to do is press button B to hear the gratifying chink of coins cascading into the metal cup beneath the slot. I head for the operational kiosk.

"Hello?"

(Pause)

"Is that Galloway the Grocers?"

(Brief pause)

"Can I speak to John, please?"

(Longer pause)

"Hello ...hello ...Is that John? The van driver? This is The Hawk from Hawkhead speaking."

(Snorts and muffled laughter from the other end)

"Listen, pal, you've got to make the pick up tonight ... something's come up."

(Pause)

"Midnight ...on the dot."

(Pause)

"The spot on the Barrhead Road Don ...er, my friend told you about."

(Pause)

"Oh you'll know us all right. We'll be in strips."

(Muffled laughter and grunts from John's end)

"No, not stripped. We'll not be naked. We'll be wearing football strips. My friend will be wearing a St Mirren top. Mine will be an Aston Villa – how do I describe it? – a claret and light blue Harlequin number."

(More muffled snorts and a breathless question)

"No! How dare you accuse me of that! If I wasn't so busy with a robbery in Edinburgh just now, I'd pay you a visit in Lambhill Street and break your arms for you."

(Short pause)

"Apology accepted. Just be there. At midnight. With the forty pounds."

I smash the receiver down on the cradle with some force. I'm angry, not with John, the part-time fence with the van. I'm angry with myself because I'm going to have to con my best pal.

"Mercury?" I whisper urgently into the mouthpiece of the phone in the kiosk in Gower Street. "This is The Hawk speaking. Listen, we're going to have a dress rehearsal tonight."

(Pause)

"Relax, Mercury. We're not going to steal the boiler. I just want to check the timing. You know how I love statistics and writing things down, don't you? This is what professional robbers call a dry run. We'll load that monster on to a wheelbarrow I've stashed near the greenhouses. I'll bring my ma's clothesline and we'll rig the boiler to the barrow. I'm allowing us exactly thirty-five minutes to wheel the load down to the iron gate on the Barrhead Road that's at the end of the path coming down from the hospital main buildings."

(Pause)

"No, no, no, Mercury. We'll wheel it back up to the mortuary. Depending on the timings, I'll maybe enlist somebody else to give me a hand sometime in the future."

(Pause)

"Don't worry about that, Mercury. I'll get in touch with the van guy and cancel. You're in the clear, Mercury. The Hawk will never let you be placed in a situation of jeopardy."

(Pause)

"Right, at exactly eleven o'clock I'll be in your back garden. I'll whistle the first eight bars of *Hug-oireann ò-ro, gur toigh leam fhìn thu*. You'll put your St Mirren strip on and slip outside to join me. See you at eleven."

This part of the big heist goes smoothly enough. Big Donald, dressed for a game of football at Love Street, isn't exactly enthusiastic.

"You serious about bringing the boiler back?"

"Of course."

"We'll get caught."

"Doubt it. Who'd catch us?"

"Who? Someone who's keeping watch on the Mortuary during the hours of darkness and isn't keen on us taking their copper."

"I can live with that risk, Mercury. All I want to do is find out how long it will take us to complete the whole operation." We are taking the long way round the hospital grounds, heading due south towards the farm where Alex Orr, the Ileach, worked as an orraman. (Alex Orr was a Gaelic singer whom we had often heard at the Govan Ceilidh, which was held in the Cardell Halls every Thursday night.)

In this roundabout way we got to the Mortuary at exactly 11.35. My late father's eighteen carat pocket watch, which I was to pawn a few years later, was dangling round my neck on an Albert chain, grazing the quartered blue and claret of my football top. After consulting it, I looked skyward as we stood in front of the boiler.

"What are you looking for?" Big Donald asks.

"Just making sure nobody's spying on us from the mortuary roof."

"So there's nobody watching?" Donald says.

"No."

"So it's definitely happening then?"

"Happening."

It is very dark on a moonless night. With difficulty I locate the wheelbarrow next to the greenhouses and wheel it back to where Big Donald is standing, legs apart, behind the boiler. I assume the Sumo wrestler's position on the side opposite Donald. The idea is to lift the boiler and deposit it sideways across the barrow and then secure it with loops of rope for safe transportation to the arranged meeting point.

"*Phiosteaga, Phiosteaga,*" I shout to my pal, re-iterating how the old man MacPhee encouraged his dog to attack the otherworldly woman who was pursuing him with a knife in the tale of 'The Sheiling of the Single Night. "*Ma rinn thu riamh e, dèan an-nochd e,* If you ever did it before, be sure to do it tonight." I know Big

Donald will get the allusion. As we bend our knees and hug the huge middle expanse of the boiler we will be spurred to greater efforts.

"Right, Mercury. After three. One ...(inhale deeply) Two ... (inhale) ...Three! Aaaarrgh, aaarrgh, aaarrgh." The boiler does not budge.

"We could give it another go," Big Donald says.

"No, Mercury ...the ball ...is definitely ...on the slates."

(This saying is derived from street football. When a careless defender punts the tennis ball high above the adjacent tenement roof to have it roll back to lodge in the gutter, this puts a stop to play until some daredevil can be persuaded to risk his life to clamber through a loft door and then through a skylight window to retrieve it, or until another ball can be obtained. When 'the ba' is on the slates' it means effectively 'game over'.)

"We going home now?" Big Donald asks.

"No. I'm not concerned about this boiler – I mean, I don't mind admitting that the thing was too heavy to move. I'm concerned, I don't want to alarm you, Mercury. What I'm telling you is, this van guy ...Willie, is it? ... no, John ...he's tied up with some really bad big gangsters. They're like slashing people who cross them. They like going to war and stuff like that."

"What are we going to do?"

"I mean, this is a shock, obviously. But, Mercury, we can recover."

"How?"

"By you running down to the back gate and being ready to flag down the Galloway's van as soon as you see it ...at the stroke of midnight."

"How do you know the guy'll be passing the back gate at midnight?"

"I don't know for sure. But these mad gangsters are always looking to make a quick quid, and, for all I know, they've made a point of having the van-guy drive along Barrhead Road every night at twelve o'clock."

"Why don't we both go down to the gate?"

"He knows you … like, you've spoken to him face to face, Mercury.

"And what will you be doing while I'm down there?"

"Securing the crime scene. I know, I know, there's not going to be any crime, but I'll keep cop watch until you come back. Just tell him The Hawk's got another buyer, and he's busy casing the bank job in Edinburgh. It's better if you're the messenger."

"What's the time?" Big Donald asks.

I consult my father's watch. "Quarter to twelve. Should take you about five minutes, walking quickly. Just do it, Mercury."

"Okay." The big fellow turns and saunters off into the darkness.

With my hands on the handles of the barrow I lower by body, face down into its rather shallow interior. My shins are sticking over the edge and my feet are well clear of the implement. I have a terrific idea. I'll do press-ups. I've decided to do something that will make me stronger during the time that it takes Big Donald to get me off the hook.

I start doing the push-ups very slowly and I'm aware that the scene would look very weird if you filmed it from the side. You know, a young madman in an English football top, extended bare legs ending in studded boots, raising and lowering his body inside a wheelbarrow is decidedly bizarre behaviour. I start to do them up and down – one, two, three … until I rest at fifteen. After about a five minute recovery break, I grip the handles again. One, two, three …My arms burn. My neck crinks. This set is tougher than the last. When I get to fifteen I keep going.

Badoom Badoom. Badoom

My heart is thrumming now and I feel the blood pressuring its way through me as I approach nineteen.

"*A Thormoid, dè fo thalamh tha thu a' dèanamh*, Norman, what on earth are you up to?"

The question is posed by Katie Mary, Donald's first cousin from Baleshare. She is standing, tall and blonde, in starched nurse's uniform, with a torch in her hand. I strain and discharge myself from the handles of the barrow with a final twisting leap sideways.

A strange and traumatic experience which I am reluctant to describe consists of standing in Aston Villa football kit at midnight before an older and attractive woman from Uist who has been dispatched on some errand by the ward sister. Suffice it to say that the urge to flee is powerful.

"*Chuir mi thugam mi fhìn*, I've been exerting myself," I gasp, sweat pouring down my face.

"*Chan eil thu ag ràdh*, Could have fooled me," Katie Mary says with a dismissive snort and clicks her way towards the Pavilion Ward.

The sweat has turned cold on my body by the time Big Donald gets back to the Mortuary.

"How did you get on, Mercury" I ask innocently.

"All right."

"Did the van-guy turn up?"

"Oh, yeah," Donald replies coolly.

"How did he take the knock-back?" I enquire, pretending that I'm astonished that the van turned up at midnight.

"He was cool."

"What did he say when you told him the deal was off?"

"Och," says Donald and he makes a dismissive flicking motion with the fingers of his right hand to indicate the patronizing attitude of the van-guy. "All he said before he floored the accelerator peddle was, 'Whit do you expect? You're just a couple of Hectors.'

Slowly, slowly we walk back to Donald's home in Crookston Road. I try to tell my friend that in the big, bad world outside the bubble of Gaelic speakers everyone is a user and everyone is a resource. We are no different. Much, much later I changed my tune.

I intend to spend what's left of the night in the house of Donald's parents, Big Calum MacRitchie, from Cross Skigersta, Ness, and his wife *Raonaid Sheumais Bhàin* from Baleshare, North Uist. No, I have no intention of going to my own home in Brand Street. I have no thought of my mother who trundles night and day on the Singer Sewing Machine to earn money as a seamstress. I look on my wee uncle Colin who lodges with us and who shares a bed with me 'ben the room' as somebody to whom I am in no way accountable. My wee sister, Lorna? She's just a wee smout whom I ignore for most of the time. I possess the keys of the flat now and I've taken to coming and going as I please.

A GLIMPSE OF THE VIPER'S FANGS

Coming and going as I please, toing and froing, restless travel, strange beds, stranger companions, the rage against God – all this is to be the story arc of my life for the next fifty seven years.

I am looking at the words 'as I please' and I suddenly freeze. My hands, drooping from slack wrists over the keyboard in the Bride of Frankenstein position, are incapable of movement. I lean forward, hunching my shoulders. I sense my eyes are opening very wide, as though taking in a vista too vast to comprehend. And it is a vista that goes back fifty-seven years.

Truth be told, although I look back on some aspects of my life with affection, I do not commend it as a template for others. In the first sixteen years of my life, I suppose I functioned reasonably well. I do admit I was becoming increasingly fascinated by drug alcohol and, even at the age of sixteen, I discerned, one or two miles down the road, disturbing visions. During the years between 1953 and 1957, my journey towards fully-fledged alcoholism was a leisurely saunter from gentle uplands towards the gothic, haunted house perched on the mountaintop. It was my desire to explore this citadel, built obviously by a graduate of the

Norman Bates School of Architecture, from which low screams and grunts issued, and which featured with increasing frequency in my dreams. I was fascinated by the gaunt ruin on the hillside and I marched purposefully towards it. Little did I know that I would enter this dwelling in my twenties and sentence myself to over fifty years in this grim prison.

My first admission to a psychiatric unit for alcohol abuse was in late October 1964 and that first admission to the Ross Clinic in Aberdeen formed the basis of a pattern. Unfortunately, this was the experience I tried to replicate on more than fifty occasions at detox wards in various psychiatric hospitals in UK and the US thoughout the following forty-six years. I'd drink myself into a state of physical and mental decrepitude, invite intervention, get wheeched off to a hospital setting and abstain from ingesting alcohol for periods of varying duration after discharge.

This was my coping device for decades. Life getting tough? Relationships becoming fraught? Flee from reality through alcohol. Seek temporary surcease in hospital. Then go through the same sequence again. My acceptance of the ordinary, boring, unvarying regularity of this downward spiral throughout almost all of my adult years is a baffling mystery to me today.

Why does anyone drink? From boredom, loneliness, habit, hedonism, lack of self-esteem; as stress relief, a short-cut to adventure; to muffle the past, obliterate the present, escape to the future. Obviously I can't say this with great authority, but I think drugs and alcohol for me were a shut-the-system-down thing. I was a kind of joyless drinker. I just used bevvy for anaesthesia. When I was really young I had this image of the Gael as somebody who lived hard and drank hard. This was the cultural model I fell for. Maybe I was just addicted to risk.

My last hospital admission was in 2010 when I ended up in *Ospadal Uibhist agus Bharraigh* for ten days, after engaging in another push-pull debate with alcohol. For me at least, I hope and pray that there will be no more butting heads with that toxic dichotomy.

This is not a digression: I'm veering off-piste to tell of a weird incident. In the eighth round of the second boxing match for the Middleweight Championship of the world between Sugar Ray Leonard and the Panamanian Roberto (Hands of Stone) Duran on November 25, 1980 in New Orleans an incredible thing happened. Duran turned away from Leonard and uttered the two most famous words in boxing history: No mas. He had quit the ring, a huge no-no. No one knew exactly what had happened and that probably remains true today.

I, Tormod, re-iterate the words old 'Hands of Stone': no more. No one, including me, knows exactly what happened in April 2010. I quit. I finally owned up to who I was and admitted, like Jonah of old, that it was necessary to proceed in a new direction.

JOB AND FINISH

Well, sin agaibh ur cuid, that's your whack. As my late father used to say upon the completion of any task, 'Job and finish.'

Taing dhan Tighearna, Thank the Lord, the horror of my bondage to drug alcohol is behind me. I am now on the better side of a dividing line in my life. By the grace of God, and the love and support of friends, I have recovered from being a poor, drunken wreck the way you do from a virus: suspiciously, gingerly, gratefully, not wanting to be too presumptuous. I still struggle with many temptations, but I know that something has changed within me. My priorities are different. I've lowered the temperature, the heat and the need. My life these days has structure and purpose. The God I raged against has brought me up out of the pit.

ACKNOWLEDGEMENTS AND APOLOGIES

Thanks to Iain Townsend, a man who came of age in the Twitter era. His verdict on a first draft chapter was: 'Interesting, but too long.' I shortened the chapters. A particular debt of gratitude is also owed to Mike and Peigi Townsend, to Maighread, Malcolm and 'Teddy' Simpson, to Jamie Chambers and Fraser Macdonald, and to my daughter, Temora, for reasons that need not be explained here. With regard to the latter, I reiterate my sincere apologies for the hurt caused to herself, and to her mother, Moira, by my folly.